A House Alive with Words

A House Alive with Words

*Stories from the ABC Program,
a path to college for inner-city youth*

PATRICIA ZITA KRISCH
with Jason S. Fritz

DEASON PRESS
Philadelphia   2015

DEASON PRESS
www.deasonpress.com

Cover photograph by Sharon Sherman
Cover design by Miriam Seidel

Library of Congress Control Number: 2015904668
ISBN 978-0-9908306-0-3

For the eight young men who so generously shared their stories

Contents

Foreword

The longer that I remain as an active member of my profession, the more people ask me questions about how to save public education in the city. It's as if my graying hair and experience in some of our country's most high achieving schools qualifies me to expound with authority on a complex set of issues that have long perplexed far more knowledgeable people who have studied and researched urban education.

I began as a teacher in a forgotten part of Philadelphia and, like most young people, I was ready to save the world. After all, I had been a very well liked counselor at an overnight camp for city kids located in the exurbs of the same city, and I had teacher certification from a well-respected college of education. I was also naïve and a product of white privilege.

To sum up my five-year teaching experience: I was a miserable failure. The harder I worked, the more frustrated I became. Any gains in student performance and behavior that I might observe, would quickly disappear over the weekend or during extended vacations. The thirty hours that I spent each week with my twelve-year-olds couldn't trump the one hundred and thirty hours when they were under the influence of other variables. I didn't know then and still do not know today how to beat those odds without a change in environment.

As I look back at my own camp experience, as I have observed the success stories of young people who have attended residential programs including boarding school, and as I have both observed and heard the testimonials of alumni from *A*

Better Chance programs, I am convinced that there are models and methods that need to be replicated and expanded.

Removing young people from loving homes and from what they know best, even for a temporary period, is not without its own set of issues. However, I am convinced that removing, or at least reducing, the innate fears that are part of everyday living in a child's environment is more important and may be the only hope that we have of helping most young people reach their potential.

My experience with *A Better Chance* spans a period of over 30 years in three public school districts in the suburbs of Philadelphia and New York. Their results are impressive. But even more important than the quality of the teaching and the quality of the schools to which the students have been assigned, is the commitment of the adults who work with these students. These students' better chance is due to the support they receive from committed adults who create conditions that make for a safe and inclusive community.

Patty Krisch is one of those adults who has made a difference by supporting A Better Chance in Ardmore, Pennsylvania. How fortunate she was to have been so involved with the young men profiled herein and at a *House Alive with Words!*

DAVID W. MAGILL, ED.D.
Director of the University of Chicago
Laboratory Schools (2003 to 2014)
Superintendent of Schools,
Lower Merion School District (1991 to 2002)

Introduction

In my first job as a graduate student in sociology at the University of Chicago, I worked on a study of teenaged gang members who lived in inner-city Chicago. As a young white woman from Sacramento, California, I was both enthralled and shocked to learn of the texture of life for poor fourteen-, fifteen- and sixteen-year-olds. And I was saddened to learn how easily the possibility of good life chances can disappear: a gang fight leaving someone shot, a strong armed robbery that escalated and turned fatal, a teenager sentenced to jail at fifteen. Although I moved on to work in another area of sociology, the stories I heard in that job never left me; regret over wasted lives stayed with me.

Decades later, when I was asked to join the board of A Better Chance in Lower Merion in 1994, I gladly accepted. Here was a chance to work with boys, many of them from the same kind of circumstances of those gang members, and to help them create different life outcomes for themselves.

The ABC in Lower Merion takes academically talented but economically disadvantaged boys of color and houses them together for four years while they attend Lower Merion High School. This school, in the affluent Main Line suburbs of Philadelphia, ranks high in terms of SAT scores, number of National Merit Semifinalists, and various other measures of excellence. Our ABC program provides supervision, tutoring and support. The students receive full scholarships, which include room and board, a weekly allowance and trips home for major holidays. Normally eight students at a time are in the program, guaranteeing a lively house chockfull of teenagers.

This program is a part of the national organization, A Better Chance. Since its founding in 1963, over 14,000 teenaged boys and girls of color whom A Better Chance has placed have graduated from private prep schools, independent day schools and public schools. Most of the students go on to graduate from college. Over ninety young men have graduated from ABC in Lower Merion since it was started in 1973. Financial support comes entirely from people in the community.

Our ABC House is located on a tree-shaded street that is a mixture of small apartment buildings and single-family homes. A senior center sits next door. The Ardmore Community Center (known as the Shack), which primarily serves the African American residents in the nearby historically black part of Ardmore, is across the street. Shooting baskets there lets the ABC students get to know the kids in the neighborhood. The commercial center of Ardmore, with shops and restaurants, lies within an easy walk from the ABC House, and the boys frequently head there to a Rite Aid and a McDonald's.

The ABC in Lower Merion students live, along with four staff members, in a large, white three-story house in Ardmore. The house, originally built as a rooming house, has public areas and one student bedroom on the first floor, with more student bedrooms on the second floor. The public areas and the boys' rooms are furnished with what one boy described as furniture "that looks like it can take a real beating." The staff members live on the third floor or in an attached apartment.

At the time of the events in this book two resident directors managed the day-to-day aspects of the program and two residential staff tutors, who were usually recent college graduates, ran the five-nights-a-week required study hall. Staff members typically attend graduate school or work at day jobs, and must balance being authority figures, role models and friends, all the while having little privacy because they live with their charges. Staff and students gather for dinner together every weeknight at six o'clock for a meal prepared by a part-time cook.

As a board member for the past twenty years, I have gone with boys to teacher conferences and doctor's appointments, watched them at high school football and basketball games, cheerleading competitions and musical productions, and have attended art shows. I have baked acres of brownies. I have prodded, cajoled and sometimes tutored them in their schoolwork. I have struggled to help boys in crises, some of which jeopardized their continuing in the program. I have listened to them talk about serious issues and I have enjoyed seeing the sheer silliness that a houseful of boys ages fourteen to nineteen can produce. I have celebrated the acceptance of these boys into excellent colleges.

Several years ago, Hayat Omar and Jay Fritz, both part of our staff at that time, began holding poetry readings with whatever students were hanging around the house on Friday and Saturday evenings. Soon many of the students were writing and reading their own poems. Hayat arranged for the boys to do a reading of their poems before the board, and this became an annual event. Realizing that their poems are a gateway to understanding the experiences and challenges our ABC scholars face, Jay and I decided to undertake this book. Together we began, and then I continued taping hours and hours of interviews with the boys. The stories they told us, and our own interactions with them, form the core of this book, which could not have been written without their enthusiastic participation.

Cast of Characters

JONATHAN
*from the Bronx, New York,
and Pittsfield, Massachusetts*

ELVIS
from Brooklyn, New York

EDWIN
from Inwood Manhattan, New York

TYRELL
from Brooklyn, New York

ANTHONY
from Baltimore, Maryland

PETER
from Hartford, Connecticut

MICHAEL (not his real name)
from Brooklyn, New York

CHARLES (not his real name)
from Brooklyn, New York

CHAPTER 1

Getting In

Jonathan: A Better Chance

Early in his sixth-grade year in a middle school in the South Bronx, Jonathan finally discovered a solution to his problems: he quit school.

He was sick of bullies, sick of spitballs thrown at him in class, sick of being bumped, shoved, teased and hassled. Being in school was hard enough, but getting home safely was worse. "I had to walk by some hot spots. I'd try to go around where everybody was."

One day he just decided not to go to school. He found this easy to hide from his mother, who had to leave for work at five in the morning. His brother also left for a different school before Jonathan did. Jonathan would get up and get dressed as if for school and, after everyone left, he'd go back to bed and sleep, and later watch TV. "I'd make my own little homework assignments." As he told me this, Jonathan waved an imaginary piece of paper in the air. "So if she asked, I'd say 'here it is.'"

This idyll lasted for forty-five days.

Then his mother got a letter from the school telling her that not only was he not in school, he was failing the first quarter. Jonathan denied it. "I thought, go ahead and try to prove it. I didn't think she would." But the next day his mother went to the school and found out he was lying.

"My mom was yelling at me. She was mad!" After a long, long talk, Jonathan went back to school and, "basically just sucked it up. I hated it, hated it."

Back at school, he tried a new tactic with the bullies: he sometimes did homework for them when they told him to. At first he thought it might provide him with protection. But it didn't, so he just endured.

Jonathan, who is on the short side, said, "I remember being so scared when the bell rang. I knew that once we got out of school, I'd have to have my guard up—be careful going around every single corner because there'd be grocery stores. The gangs were usually there or by the projects." He was afraid of getting jumped—which did happen a couple of times. An adult from the neighborhood came each time and rescued him by yelling at the gang members.

Even going to the grocery store around the corner from home was dangerous. When he had to go, he would rush back as quickly as he could. Mostly he stayed in the apartment. Jonathan and his family had moved into the South Bronx when he was just starting middle school, so none of the teenagers in the neighborhood knew him. "I was just a random kid."

Jonathan missed so much of sixth grade that he had to repeat it. In seventh grade, his history teacher singled him out for encouragement, and convinced him that if he worked hard, he could have a better life. He decided to try. He liked the attention he got from his teachers and the pride his mother showed in him. "In eighth grade I decided to go all out. I just studied, studied, studied."

By eighth grade most of the bullies had done what Jonathan had tried in sixth grade—they disappeared. His English teacher, recognizing a bright and motivated student, told him about ABC and encouraged him to apply.

In spite of what these two teachers did to encourage him, Jonathan came perilously close to not getting into an ABC program. He took a standardized test, wrote essays, filled out required forms, gave forms to teachers to fill out and waited to hear from ABC. And waited and waited. His school guidance counselor, who was supposed to coordinate the school's part of his application, had gone on maternity leave. Jonathan's application sat on her desk for all the months she was on leave. When she came back to work, she sent it on—but the deadline had passed. However, the person at the national ABC office who was responsible for sending applications to member programs recognized something especially promising in Jonathan, and asked us to consider him. His standardized test scores were not remarkable; but trusting her judgment, we invited him to come for an interview. Impressed with his motivation and articulateness, our committee held a quick discussion after the interview and offered him a position before he left town rather than wait the usual day or two to discuss it in detail.

Over the years I became especially close to Jonathan, with his almond-shaped eyes and distinctive laugh, and I took over as his academic advisor for his last two years of high school. Still, it was not until he was a senior that he told me he found me to be scary at his interview. Startled by this, I asked him why. "You asked me a really challenging question. I thought you were a very tough person."

I asked Jonathan when he had gotten over being scared of me, and he said it was when I hired him one day to help in my garden. I had planted a cottage garden, which requires way more work than I can manage on my own. For years I hired a few ABC boys at a time on some weekends to come help me as I worked alongside them. Jonathan had a lot of fun the first time he came over, and decided I was okay.

Even though Jonathan was eager to come to an ABC program, he faced a bundle of challenges his first year with us. In spite of this, he said about coming to Ardmore, "I could tell at night when I would walk to West Coast Video, I just felt sooo much safer because I knew that there weren't any gangs around. And I knew that if something happened to me, there were people to watch over me: the guys in the house and the staff. I feel lighter. Walking, I didn't feel that danger anymore."

Coming to ABC: Elvis

The boys who come to ABC in Lower Merion arrive with a dream in their heads and an even bigger dream in their hearts. Rarely are they challenged to articulate those dreams, but one fall night the staff announced they had a special program to present after our monthly board meeting. They had told each boy to write a short essay about what being in the program meant to him. One by one, the boys got up and read their pieces.

When Elvis, who was then a sophomore, took his turn, he read an essay about his middle school teacher, Mr. Rivera. With much emotion, he recounted how one day this teacher had told his class that according to some statistics he had seen, probably only one percent of them would graduate from a four-year college. "It hurt Mr. Rivera to see such numbers because he dreamt that so much more would become of us." After we accepted Elvis into our ABC, Mr. Rivera told him that he stood the best chance of being that one percent, if he kept focused.

Elvis had learned about ABC from his Brooklyn middle school guidance counselor. The counselor urged him to apply, saying it would be a chance to attend one of the best schools in America. Elvis had applied in fifth grade for a scholarship to a Catholic school in Manhattan, and then in sixth grade to Hunter College's Middle School, but didn't get accepted into either of them. He told me, "I was definitely interested."

In sixth grade, Elvis had attended George Gershwin Junior High School, a school that was rife with gang activity. As a young adult looking back, Elvis described in detail his memories of that challenging year. His experience vividly reflects a background shared by many ABC students, conveying the intensity and stress felt by a young teen trying to navigate the everyday dangers of living in a community where violence is a given, and gangs hold sway.

Elvis's mother had made clear to him that he had to be a fighter. "My mom told me early on that if anyone hit me, I was to hit that person back because at all costs I could not be a punk. . . . I must fight to win, and if I ever came home crying from being bullied or losing a fight, I would get my ass whooped by her." He wasn't raised to be a bully, but told it was important to know when to fight. On the first day of sixth grade, he had his first encounter, when another boy waiting for the bus threw a vulgar insult of Elvis's mother at him—a known breach of the code he followed. "I jumped up, grabbed his skull with my left hand, and punched him several times with the other hand." When questioned by a school aide, he explained the other boy's provocation, and was let go without punishment. The incident "gave me a bit of a reputation as someone not to cross the line with," Elvis explained.

Soon, however, an innocent after-school friendship with a girl in his neighborhood led to his first run-in with a local gang. A gang leader approached Elvis with the girl in tow, and warned him to stay away from her. "It was a tough situation to read," he remembered. Since the gang member hadn't provoked him with insults, Elvis chose not to respond. But from that point on, the other boy, accompanied by "his goons," kept harassing him: "He'd make an appearance; interrupt basketball games, just playing mind games." Elvis tried to rally a group of kids with a shared antipathy to the gang, making a boastful play on the gang's name. But he soon realized the others were too scared to back him up. And his bragging came back to haunt him.

On the basketball court one day, Elvis found himself surrounded by the gang members, questioning him about his insult to their gang name. Elvis knew he was in danger. "I had to be smart. I had to swallow my pride in front of my acquaintances on the basketball court. I had to lie to save myself. 'No, I never said those things. What is being said about you guys never came from me. Those are lies.' Saying those things showed everyone that I was afraid of them, and that fit perfectly with their aura. I saved myself a group beating by eating my words, but discredited myself as to what I thought at the time it meant to be a man."

The gang's petty harassment continued, and was taken up by their smallest member. One day while Elvis sat in class, the other boy stood at the door, pointing and mocking him from behind the glass. "I got right out from my seat and ran over to the door. The little Napoleon dashed down the hallway out of sight. I did not pursue him further." To Elvis, the boy had crossed the line: as an A student, Elvis had always kept his classroom behavior separate from the constant low-level warfare of school and after-school life. "No one ever crossed my path to where it took attention away from my schoolwork." He knew he had to put an end to this situation.

He got his chance when the boy with the Napoleon complex showed up in the school hallway, while Elvis was play wrestling with friends and accidently hurt one of them causing the boy to cry. "Napoleon" grabbed the friend's hand and used it to smack Elvis. "I pushed him to the ground, pinned his arms with my knees so I would have free range to his face. I got in a few clear punches. The fight was fast, and . . . I did not realize that his whole group formed and tried kicking me while I beat their friend." Elvis felt proud afterward, in spite of a bloody fist—"Napoleon had braces"—and some bumps on his head. But even this victorious moment brought an aftermath filled with moral ambiguity for a sixth-grader. Sent to the dean, he decided he had to stay quiet about the gang's involvement; snitching would put him in danger of consequences that the school might not be able to prevent.

Later, the gang tried to claim that Elvis had been beaten in the fight. But he avoided more altercations with them. "I did not care to go and prove myself a second time. The purpose of the fight had been fulfilled—the harassment stopped." Once that school year was over, Elvis transferred back to his area middle school.

Seventh grade proved a turning point for him. "My mother told me the very first day that if I got into a fight she would beat me. This contradicted everything she had taught me before, but her message was clear—as I was further maturing, there'd be more consequences for fighting. From that point on I had to use words. I had to intimidate without fighting because I already knew I was tough and had the body to avoid most troublemakers."

Elvis lived in a three-bedroom apartment in Brooklyn in a mostly Latino neighborhood with his mother, father, an older sister, a younger sister and a brother eleven years Elvis's junior. His family had moved a few times, mostly within a small area.

His father raised pigeons on the roof as a hobby. Elvis's major chore at home was to clean out the pigeon coop; he also helped his father construct coops. Immigrants from Puerto Rico, his father's family had lived in an old apartment building with just an open space between two adjoining buildings, where people used to throw their trash. The man who lived in the next apartment would keep the pigeons he was raising in that space, and Elvis's dad, when he was growing up, liked to reach out the window and try to grab the pigeons. Elvis doesn't know if his father ever caught one of them, but ever after he wanted to raise pigeons. Sharing care of the pigeons fostered a bond between Elvis and his father.

I first met Elvis one September, when I dropped by the ABC House on the afternoon the new students were moving in. I have a vivid memory of walking up the concrete pathway to the house and seeing a large, broad-shouldered boy, Elvis, and his mother sitting on a bench just to the side of the front steps. I crossed the beaten front lawn to greet them and introduce myself. That year, as every year, I remembered how it used to feel leaving my daughter at summer camp in the care of strangers—and that was only for four weeks. How hard it must be for mothers to leave their fourteen-year-old sons with us, knowing it would be for the entire school year.

I invited them to come inside with me for an informal meeting with a few board members and the four staff members. There we talked to the new students and their parents about the program, and about what to expect for the next few days. The staff had planned many activities, including a treasure hunt, as a way for them to learn their way around the neighborhood.

Elvis had spent the summer before coming to ABC helping out at his father's hot dog stand. "My parents kept lecturing me about keeping my room clean because they'd seen how messy the other guys' rooms were. Also, they made it sound sort of like jail. They told me, 'put your name on everything: your clothes, your sheets.'"

What Elvis remembers most about the trip coming to ABC was, "We were packing up the car and I had on the first pair of Timberland boots I ever had. They were too big for me. By the time we got to Ardmore I was trying to perfect my walk in them. And I saw Ned [not his real name] and he says, 'what's up my brother?' and I didn't know what to say."

When I was leaving the ABC House that first day I saw Elvis's mother standing on a chair in his room measuring the three tall windows, which faced north. A couple of weeks later, mother-made curtains arrived.

After his parents left, he went into the first-floor bedroom he would share with a sophomore who was not set to arrive for a few days. Alone in the large, high-ceilinged room, he lay on his bed looking out the windows to a long driveway edged by a metal fence. He felt excited, happy, free of a lot of home responsibilities. The more he thought about the adventure he was embarking on, the more excited he felt. He stood up on the bed and started jumping, up and down, up and down—till he heard a thud. He'd broken a bedspring. *I'm in big trouble,* he thought. Then he thought, I'd better not tell anyone. "No one found out I did it, but I did have to sleep on that broken spring all year long."

Hello, I'm Michael

The first time I met Michael (not his real name, and some identifying details have been omitted) he made a remarkable impression. A few weeks after school started one fall, our program hosted a social event at the ABC House for board members, host families, academic advisors, and of course the students. As I walked down the long, broad front hall, I saw a slender African American teen standing at a little table. As I approached he stuck out his hand, introduced himself and asked me to fill out a nametag to wear. I have never before or since had such an experience at the house.

Thinking that a staff member had decided this was a good way for this freshman to meet members of the ABC family, I complimented them on it. Wrong, they told me. It was entirely Michael's idea. I felt as if the ghost of my father, who could work a room with overflowing Irish charm, had reappeared in the form of an inner-city boy from Brooklyn.

This first impression augured perfectly for how Michael would get along with the many, many adults who volunteer with the ABC program. Michael, who joined us along with two other freshmen—Elvis, and another who did not make it past his first year—came from a somewhat more financially secure background than most of the other ABC boys did. His mother was a schoolteacher in New York City. Although Michael lived primarily with her and her partner, he had extensive family ties on both of his parents' sides.

Michael particularly liked to talk about his grandmother's house in Brooklyn. "People ask what do you do in the city compared to here. In the city I could sit on my grandmother's porch for hours, me and my cousins, and see things happening in front of me. Here you see snow, you see cars driving by."

Every few blocks in his Brooklyn neighborhood were either Crips' or Bloods' territory. The middle school he attended had mostly Crips. Sometimes the Bloods would come after school and the kids in the two gangs would fight, but Michael said he never felt really afraid. Michael was careful not to wear gang colors, and used the phrase, 'I'm NFL,' meaning neutral for life.

Each spring an ABC committee interviews prospective students for the program. For four years, the chair of the committee asked the sociable and articulate Michael to be one of two student members on it. Each time he was called on to describe what a typical day for an ABC student is. Talking with Michael for our book, I asked him to recreate what he usually said to them.

"A typical day in the morning, you get up around six o'clock, six-thirty, depending on how long it takes you to get ready. Me? I usually get up about six forty-five. I roll out of bed to the bus stop.

"The bus picks us up at Spring and Ardmore Avenue at seven.

"We eat breakfast in school. You have the option of eating here but you have to get up even earlier. We are ABC students and we get free breakfast in school, too.

"Homeroom starts at seven thirty-five. That lasts for about ten minutes.

"Then you go to your first period class. Go through the motions of the day. The first eight periods.

"If you don't do any sports or other school activities, you are home by about two forty-five on the bus which drops you off at Ardmore and Spring. If you have sports you might come home at five-thirty after practice. If you have a game, you might come home a little later.

"We have dinner here at six o'clock. Dinner lasts about twenty minutes so is done by about six-twenty. Study hall starts at seven, ends at nine-thirty, everyday from Sunday to Thursday.

"Bedtime's at eleven."

Michael would often tell prospective students, "Forget about TV. Your favorite programs come during study hall." (I've noticed, however, that watching TV is a favorite pastime during the afternoon, especially on bad weather days.)

I asked him, "When do you do laundry?"

"We each have an assigned laundry day. Me and Elvis share a laundry day and our day is Monday. It usually goes by roommates. Some people do it before study hall, finish after study hall; some do it right after you come home from school. There's no shower schedule. Whoever gets there first."

I asked, "What do you do between dinner and study hall?"

"Might take a shower. Some people get on the computer, IM. If you have a lot of work, you might start something earlier. Once it is better weather outside than right now we might play a quick game of basketball or baseball or whatever."

Michael doesn't usually tell the prospective students what they do after study hall, but I have been there enough times to know the drill. At nine-thirty the house comes alive. Most boys first make a beeline to the kitchen for heavy-duty snacking. They might heat up leftovers from dinner or eat them cold. They might stick a Pop Tart or a slice of frozen pizza in the microwave. If the cook has made a cake or pies, they'll tuck into that. Often board members have dropped off cookies, donuts or cake. After the enforced quiet, or at least the attempt at quiet during study hall, there is lots of chatter, often loud, in the kitchen.

After refueling, some boys go back to the computer room to finish a paper or study for a test, or they may head upstairs to their rooms to continue with homework. Staff members can usually predict which boys will do that. Others troll the Internet for fun and instant messaging online. A few plop on the living room couches and turn on the TV or play a video game. Some evenings, two or three boys, usually the younger ones, more or less bounce off the walls: shouting, chasing around, wrestling, rolling around the floor like puppies. The one constant from nine-thirty until bedroom curfew is noise, lots of it.

Chatty Michael was often a part of it.

CHAPTER 2

Longing for Home

Edwin: Li'l Brother

For three years, from 2000 to 2003, two young poets, Hayat Omar and Jason (Jay) Fritz, were staff members at the ABC House, living with the boys, and having responsibility for their daily welfare. Jay had just graduated from Haverford College, where he majored in English and creative writing. Hayat, a small, slight woman, had earned a master's degree in social work from Bryn Mawr College and had written poetry since she was a young child in Ethiopia. Both of them encouraged the boys to express their thoughts in the form of poems. Soon they discovered that the boys were writing poems about serious themes in their lives: dreams for the future, not fitting in, longing for family, getting into trouble, and love. Lots of poems about love. In the spring of 2001, Hayat organized a poetry reading to be given before the entire house and the ABC board members. It proved to be such an emotionally satisfying evening that the staff decided to make it a yearly event.

Each year one poem grabbed the audience's attention in a way they could not easily shake. In 2003 it was Edwin's. That April evening the students, the four staff members and about twenty ABC board members filled the house living room—sitting on couches and chairs or on the floor, or standing in doorways while they listened to each boy stand and read his poem.

Small-boned and slender, Edwin, just turned fifteen, was the youngest boy in the program and the only freshman that year. Normally an outgoing boy with plenty to say, now he stammered, as he got ready to read: "I wrote my poem for my little brother. Today is his birthday, and I'm not there." Although Edwin writes graceful, Standard English prose, he wrote his poem in the street vernacular of his Dominican neighborhood in New York City.

This One's 4 U

How does one begin to talk
A person as special as you?
A person who brings you joy
& happiness along with meanings of life
which are so true

A person that makes you feel like
Every day upcoming, u start ur life anew,
Well lil bro, lemme just start by
Saying that this one's 4 u

The paper fluttered in his trembling hands. Edwin, black-eyed with a rich caramel complexion, continued.

It saddens me 2 realize that 4 ur B-day
This year, things r going to be a lil different.
That 4 the 1st time I'm not gonna be
Around 4 u when ur most happy with eyes
Full of joy & innocence.
With so much love in ur heart for those
Who sometimes don't even care to listen
This one's 4 u

About this point, Edwin choked up. He swiped an arm across his eyes, but kept reading.

Hurts every time when I ask about u
And how u doing in town

And I hear that u sad, dragging urself
& moping around
hurts every time momma tells me that
u 2 burst into tears together, cuz
u still feel as if u lost me 4 ever.

I sat riveted. As board members we concentrate on the opportunities we provide to disadvantaged youth: the chance to attend an excellent suburban high school and help in getting into college. But if life at home was happy, how hard it must be to leave it for here. This is the price our boys pay to get a decent education.

I know it's hard when we wake up
Every morning remember that we're
2 hrs away from each other.
But just promise me that you'll take care of urself,
Don't do nothing stupid, and always love me like ur brotha

Executive Board chair Rob Howard's nine-year-old daughter was sitting next to me, and now she leaned into me and whispered, "Look at my daddy. He's crying."

Edwin bowed his head, seemingly unable to read any further. I saw fellow board members squirming. A silent question—How do we rescue him from this?—ricocheted off the living room walls. "I'm all right," Edwin said as he straightened his head and soldiered on.

Just know that I'll always love u
& that this one's 4 u

Just wanna wish u the best of luck on ur special day,
And also want u 2 promise me that you'll keep on being u,
No matter what other people got 2 say.
Cuz u know if they say anything stupid,
Together we mess em up any day.

I bless the day u was born & came to me
Cuz through life there were so many things u made me see
But yo, now its time 4 me to go
Remember to always be safe if u messin wit dem hoes,
Luv u now and always,
And Antony, dis one's 4 u.

Silence. Then Hayat glided over to Edwin and gently rubbed his back. Soon Edwin's normal buoyancy returned. It was the assembled adults who stayed quiet, trying to process such raw emotion.

For weeks afterwards, board members commented to each other on how moving it was to see Edwin start to cry and then gather the poise to keep on reading. It was while reflecting on that soft April evening that Jay and I realized that the boys' poems were a gateway to recreating, at least partially, what the experience of being in ABC was like for them.

Edwin was homesick his entire freshman year: missing his younger brother, his mother, his friends and his neighborhood. However, when he returned to Ardmore for his sophomore year he seemed more at ease about being with us. He told me that during his first year he thought he was going to lose everything. However, during the summer he realized that wasn't happening. "My friends were still my friends. Everything will be the same. It's like coming out to a new world. I have two lives. I still miss home, but being at ABC is cool now."

When we talked about this, he was about to go to Costa Rica on a scholarship from the Experiment in International Living for a month in the summer. That he could do this was a good sign that he now knew he still had his home in New York to go back to and be a part of.

Edwin also had a rocky start getting into a college preparation program. When he was in the seventh grade, his school counselor recommended him for Prep for Prep, another special program. Edwin said that officials with the program told him to drop any activities he was doing over the summer because he had a good chance of getting into the program. "That summer I had plans to go to the Dominican Republic to visit family and I wanted to play baseball. So we canceled the trip and I stopped playing baseball.

"In the end they told me I wasn't going to be in the program. I cried. I went to my counselor. I didn't have a tantrum, but I was really mad. I told her, 'I don't even want to go to high school. I'm going to drop out.'

"She told me, 'Edwin, Prep for Prep is not the only program.'" She recommended him for the ABC program. "And I'm here."

Edwin explained that had he not gotten into ABC he would probably have gone to his zone high school: Kennedy. "It's like the worst high school in New York. You always hear about somebody getting stabbed. But I was going to go there because a lot of my friends go there."

Edwin had lived since he was five years old with his mother and brother in a two-bedroom apartment in a six-story building, in a Dominican neighborhood in Inwood Manhattan. Nearby are projects whose tenants are mostly black. Edwin said, "We were cool with them." They would tease each other, with the black kids saying, "'You're immigrants. You came on boats.' We'd say, 'you came on boats, too. Only thing is we decided to come here, you didn't.' We kept it friendly. If a white person had said this we'd be mad, but this was joking."

His mother, a single parent, had emigrated from rural Dominican Republic. Her English is limited and she worked long hours as a home health care worker. Edwin, black-eyed and wiry, and his younger brother spent a lot of time on the street, walking around or sitting on top of cars in front of their building chatting with their friends, or going to the nearby park to play baseball or to nearby projects to play basketball. Edwin told me everybody goes to the park in the summer and dresses up "nice" because they'd be seeing their friends.

Even so, being on the streets could be dangerous. While there were no formal gangs, sometimes fights broke out between individuals or groups. And weapons were used—people fought mostly with baseball bats, hammers, and, lately, machetes. Edwin certainly did not sound to us as if he were afraid much of the time; instead, he exuded confidence. He didn't like to fight, but if he had to, he felt he could take care of himself.

I asked him about guns. "Not many guns. The only reason to use a gun is if you want to kill somebody."

His ABC housemate, Peter, stayed with him over one Christmas break. One night they heard gunshots right outside the apartment building. The next day Edwin learned that a friend of a friend of his had been killed.

Street corners were "owned" by individual older guys who sold drugs. Edwin told me that the guys were nice to him and his friends; they were like big brothers. When I heard this, I said a silent, extra thanks that we had accepted Edwin into our program. Would Edwin, a born "people person," have been able to resist getting taken into the economy of the street at sixteen or seventeen?

A Hundred Miles Apart

Edwin was certainly not the only boy who struggled with homesickness. Jonathan had arrived in early September, fifteen years old and full of hope. Soon that hope was joined by homesickness: tears-in-the-eyes, lead-in-the-heart homesickness. A month after he arrived, we celebrated our ABC's thirtieth anniversary with a reunion weekend. As part of the festivities, we hosted a Sunday morning poetry reading for current students, alumni, and the adult ABC community. Before a roomful of adults, many of them still strangers, Jonathan, his almond-shaped eyes framed by arched eyebrows in a high forehead, stood and read a poem written to his mother.

It was you who took care of me when I was sick
And now we're a hundred miles apart

I always think about you in my sleep
Sometimes I believe you're by my side playing with my hair like
    you always did.
But no, we're a hundred miles apart.

To have the satisfaction of knowing that you will always be
    there for me
brings me to tears.
I wish you were here right now so you can take away my fears.

Not knowing what will happen next is a frightening thing
People tell me that it's going to be ok.
But they don't know what I go through each and every day.
They don't know the frustration and anger I have inside.

It's a bomb just waiting to happen
One moment everything is fine, the next, there's chaos
But eventually it will all disappear

Believe it or not I know I'm going to make it.
Whether a hundred miles or a billion.
I know you'll be by my side
I just hope this pain will subside.

I wait for the moment when we finally reunite
Maybe some day, maybe sooner than I think
Just know one thing. I never regret my decision and never will.

Jonathan struggled with homesickness all of his first year with us. This was the second time he had painfully missed his mother. While he had moved to New York from Puerto Rico with her as a baby, when he was six years old he and a slightly older brother were sent to live with their father in a small town in Puerto Rico. They lived with him until Jonathan was eleven. They were very poor, and Jonathan and his brother would sometimes knock on neighbors' doors and beg for food when they were hungry. A year after the boys returned to their mother in New York, his father died of AIDS—Jonathan had not known his father was ill.

During Jonathan's first quarter at ABC his mother, brothers and stepfather moved to Pittsfield, Massachusetts. At Thanksgiving he went home to a new town, a safer but unfamiliar environment from the South Bronx where the family had lived for several years. Instead of the two-hour bus ride home for breaks, which most of the boys took, Jonathan had to spend eight hours on the bus each way.

That first year, his moods cycled, turning on a dime from happy and outgoing to his sitting at the dinner table with his head down: not eating, not talking, enveloped in blackness. Support from several quarters helped him: host parents, staff members, a counselor, and a staff member, Tim, who gave him piano lessons. The piano lessons, although they lasted only one school year, opened up the world of music to him. Jonathan became an enthusiastic member of the school choir for his remaining three years of high school. As he made friends, did exceptionally well in his classes, and matured, he turned into a kid who was upbeat most of the time. No one will forget his frequent, distinctive laugh.

CHAPTER 3

Feeling Different

The boys in our ABC program come from inner-city neighborhoods where they are part of the dominant racial or ethnic group. They come to an upper-middle class, mostly white community and high school. How do they deal with suddenly being minorities and living in a different culture?

Charles: A Gamble

Charles (not his real name, and some identifying details have been omitted) is African American, and before coming to ABC, lived in an apartment in a three-story brownstone in Bedford-Stuyvesant with his mother, great grandmother and little sister. His mother worked for a city agency and was active in her Pentecostal church. His father sometimes lived in the area, but Charles rarely saw him.

Charles sometimes heard gunshots in the neighborhood and would hear about robberies, but he was used to it. His calm disposition probably helped him deal with these stresses. He said his mother was protective when he was "coming up." Once he turned twelve or thirteen, his mother thought it was safe enough for him to use public transit by himself. He could go to the barbershop and go shopping for clothes, and travel as far as he wanted in the city. Tall and broad-shouldered, he liked to play basketball in local leagues.

He came to ABC in a decidedly atypical way. That year, our program had no one who would be a sophomore in the coming year, and our student selection committee began actively looking for an applicant who could fill that slot. Almost all students apply to start ABC as rising freshmen, but late that spring, the national contact person sent Charles's application for us to consider. I was on the committee that year, and I remember our puzzlement. Charles was attending an automotive vocational school in Brooklyn, and he was already a high school sophomore. What was he doing applying to ABC? His grades were okay but not spectacular. However, the national ABC official felt he was worth our taking a look at. And Charles made it clear in his application that he wanted to be in an academic program.

ABC student Deashawn, then a senior, was serving as the student liaison on the selection committee. He told us that sometimes when a New York City zone school is extremely unsafe, a student elects to go to a nearby vocational school that is smaller and safer. Reassured by Deashawn's information, the committee invited Charles down for an interview. There he told us he wanted to be a lawyer, and he expressed no resistance to repeating his sophomore year in order to get into our program. We all were impressed with the grace and maturity of this teenager, who already stood at six-foot-three. We decided to take a gamble, and offered him a spot.

Many years later I asked Charles, who topped out at six-foot-six, why he first chose to go to automotive school. "That's one of those questions, I don't know," he said. "I just don't know. My grades were good. I probably would have gotten accepted to any school in New York. I always wanted to be a lawyer. My train of thought was I'll go there and I'll still go to law school and I can fix cars on the side. I could fix my own car. It was a pretty juvenile thought."

Charles's mother had struggled to pay tuition for him to attend a religiously affiliated private school from kindergarten through eighth grade. Neither Charles nor his mother realized that vocational school was not a normal route to becoming a lawyer. "I thought that even though it was a vocational school the education would be as good as anyplace else." Soon after he got to automotive school, Charles discovered he had made a huge mistake. Some of the students were there because they really were interested in learning auto repair, but more of them were just not interested in school. The school wasn't even close to where he lived; he needed to take a forty-five minute bus ride from his home. So much for Deashawn's conjecture.

A woman from the Pentecostal Christian church that Charles and his mother belonged to first told him about ABC. This woman had been an ABC student herself, and she put him in touch with an ABC national representative in New York and also helped him with the application process. Ours was the only program that invited him for an interview. He said, "When I came down, I really liked it. Everyone was so nice. There were a lot of opportunities that the public schools in New York didn't have. I wanted to come. Almost as soon as I got back, Marjorie [Merklin, then chair of the ABC student selection committee] called and offered me a position."

With his calm temperament and emotional maturity, Charles proved to be an excellent role model for the younger boys for the three years he spent at ABC. Periodically, the board members who were on the committee that accepted Charles say to each other, "Was that a good gamble or what!"

Tyrell: From a Happy Family

Tyrell and his family lived in a three-family house in Brooklyn that his grandmother owned. His family lived on the first floor in a three-bedroom apartment. He said, "It has a nice sized back yard. That's where the kids usually play." His family had moved in shortly before Tyrell and his twin sister, the youngest of five children, were born. The house, along with the happy family life inside it, provided a large measure of stability for Tyrell.

The rules at ABC did not seem strange to him because his family provided a lot of structure at home. They ate together, and he was used to having dinner at a certain time. "We could go outside and go rolling around and someone would come get us. Then we'd have to come in, wash our hands, eat dinner. The older siblings could go back out until a certain time, but the young kids after dinner, they had to go wash up, no TV. Do homework."

Being recognized in one's neighborhood played an important protective role for some of the boys. Tyrell said that when he was in junior high, he felt reasonably comfortable out on the streets, and he knew where it was safe to go. He and his twin sister and other neighborhood kids walked to and from school in a group, feeling this kept them safer. But now, "the neighborhood has gotten a lot less safe over the years. Now kids go for guns. There are street robberies, drugs and shootings."

Of his immediate neighborhood, he said that everybody knows him and respects him. He was twenty when we spoke for this book, and he felt at this age he set an example for younger kids.

Tyrell attended George Gershwin Junior High School in Brooklyn, one of two neighborhood schools in his community. His eighth grade class numbered about three hundred students. The school's population was about seventy percent black, with about twenty-five percent Hispanic and another five percent, Asian. There were no white students. Tyrell was in the school's challenge program for gifted students.

Tyrell's guidance counselor, Mr. Bernstein, a Kelsey Grammer lookalike, each year selected a few eighth graders from the school's gifted program and encouraged them to apply to A Better Chance. "He walked us through the whole process.

He told us how to fill out the application, to write the essays. He gave us practice applications and told us to hand them in to him. He gave us feedback on what to do for the real one. "Before anyone contacted me I was interested in the program. I thought if I ever go visit and don't see anything wrong with it, if they accept me, I'm going to accept. When it got toward the end of the school year and I hadn't heard from anyone, everything was set up for me to go to my neighborhood school." Then Marjorie Merklin, who was chairing the student selection committee for our board, invited him for a visit.

Tyrell's father, who was employed in a clerical position at a community hospital, drove him to Ardmore for his visit. I was impressed with the easy way his father interacted with all of the ABC boys. Someone told us that he frequently gathered up boys who lived near their home and took them along with Tyrell and his older brother to basketball practices and games. I remember that on that first visit, he was already lame from diabetic neuropathy.

Curt Wilson, the board president then, and I took Tyrell and Charles, who was also being interviewed, along with the current ABC students out for dinner. Curt, Tyrell's father and I sat at a separate table from the boisterous boys' table. During dinner his father told us that Tyrell was eager to spend part of the summer with his grandmother in Florida. His brother, a year older than Tyrell, had done this the previous summer and had returned several inches taller. Tyrell, a skinny little thirteen-year-old, was pinning his hopes on Florida. While he didn't get to Florida, by midway through his freshman year he had started to grow. Of the visit, Tyrell later told me, "When I came out to visit, right after we got home, Marjorie called. We'd only been home about a half hour. So I accepted right then and there. I didn't want to go to the high school I was going to end up in Brooklyn."

Most of our ABC students learn about the program from a teacher or guidance counselor. Mr. Bernstein's level of help and encouragement may be unusual, but many of the referring adults offer some help in a process which can be daunting for thirteen-year-olds. Of the eight students that Mr. Bernstein coached Tyrell's year, three were accepted into ABC programs, a pretty good acceptance rate for Mr. Bernstein's personal academic talent agency. Currently, only twenty percent of students who apply to ABC are placed in member schools or programs.

Suddenly in the Minority at School

During his sophomore year, our poised and sociable Michael dated a white girl briefly, until her parents objected and they broke up. This inspired him to write the following poem.

> You have told me I am not good enough.
> I have proved myself numerous times.
> But this is not good.
> I have shown you what makes me.
> You have seen what makes little Mike tick, but that's
> Not good enough for you. You don't see me for who I am you
> Just see the color of my skin, my black hair and brown eyes.
> You don't care about people, you just care
> About what kind of people.
> The color of my skin is more important
> Then the capacity of my brain.

This painful experience was new for Michael since he, like almost all of our boys, was not used to being a minority in school or in the community where he lived. De facto segregation in their inner-city schools meant that they rarely, if ever, had white students in their classes. They attended middle schools that were mostly black or mostly Latino, or a mixture of both. Suddenly, when they came to ABC they were minorities in a predominantly white, heavily Jewish public school. Black students made up about twelve percent of the students at Lower Merion, and most of them lived in the historically black section of Ardmore where the ABC House is located.

For a host of reasons, by the time that the black students who are longtime Ardmore residents reach high school, few of them are academic high achievers. And this community is a mostly lower-middle class pocket in a quite affluent upper-middle class township. Our boys don't get selected into ABC unless they have been identified as potentially high achievers. Here they are often the only non-Asian students of color in honors classes. It is a complicated mix for fourteen-year-olds to adjust to.

Michael said he didn't feel uncomfortable about this because he was expecting it. He doesn't think there are any kids who wouldn't talk to him because of his being an ABC student. He eventually made friendships at school, but none he "would consider deep." His close friends were the boys at the ABC House, and some students from Philadelphia whom he met in a community service program he took a very active part in.

He remembered only a few incidents in classes involving his race. "Right now in my environmental science class I am the only black person. I didn't notice this until someone pointed it out. We were talking about these underwater volcanoes that let out this black smoke. And someone in the class said, 'Mike!' I turned around and then I realized everybody else in the class was white except for two Asians."

I said, "He compared you to a volcano!"

Laughing, he said, "Well, to black smoke coming out." Michael didn't know if it was meant as a joke or not, but thought it probably was.

In his honors U.S. History class, discussion about affirmative action came up often in current events because that year the U.S. Supreme Court considered cases challenging the University of Michigan's admissions policies. Michael said some kids were for it, some against. He thinks that his presence in the class affected the discussion, and that some classmates refrained from saying what they thought about the issue because he was there.

"There's this one kid in my class who I don't think censors himself. I think he actually says what he means. We were talking about this game called Ghettopoly. It's like Monopoly with different streets. The point is to see how many street corners you can buy up and sell drugs, make crack houses. The cover of the box has a black person with gold teeth. In class we laughed. We talked about whether it was racist. This kid said people are too sensitive and it's not a racist game. He said people just blow things out of proportion."

Charles, with his calm, even temperament, had an easy time feeling accepted at Lower Merion. He said that he came to us following a group of ABC boys who were very popular at school, and he felt that other students looked on ABC students very favorably because of that. Also, the six-foot-plus Charles played basketball all three years he was here, which he thought helped his being accepted. Even though he had not been around many white people before, most of his friends at school were white, and he was struck by how different their culture was from what he was used to. Moreover, he said, "The local black kids at Lower Merion are different from the ones at home. The black kids here were very conscious about being black. They stay with their own group.

"The thing is, coming from Brooklyn I see it more as a cultural thing. Blacks and Dominicans will hang out together there because they share the same music, the same culture. At Lower Merion when I was in tenth grade it seemed that some of the students were not hanging out with others [because they only hung out with other black students]. It wasn't because of culture but just because they were black." He added that this seemed to vary somewhat from year to year.

Charles said about starting at Lower Merion, "Definitely going to class and being the only black face, you really notice that." Charles remembered that during his first year at Lower Merion, his English teacher showed a film of Othello where a white actor played Othello in blackface. Whenever there were discussions about race in class, he felt that he was expected to represent the whole black community. "You adjust to it but it never ceases to be uncomfortable. You feel pressed to say something intelligent." About an English teacher Charles said, "It was great to be in Dr. Hobbs's class because she is a black woman and you just feel more comfortable when you're addressing racial issues. I loved her. She was one of my favorite teachers."

Attending a mostly white school was an entirely new experience for outgoing Tyrell, who arrived from Brooklyn the same year as Charles did, but he said, "I knew what I was getting into," because he had shadowed an older ABC student when he came to Ardmore for his interview. It didn't take him long to fit in. "I'm not a shy person. I'd talk to people. They got to know me just from seeing me every day, in class, seeing me in the hallways. And it wasn't like I was the only black kid in the school." Often, however, he was the only black student in his honors classes, and he had to get used to that.

"And then I played basketball. That was good, too. The same kids I was on the freshman team with ended up on JV and the varsity with me. Even if I didn't have classes with them, I knew them from the team. Making friends was never a problem for me."

He said he also met a lot of the black students from Ardmore at "the Shack," the community center across the street from the ABC House, which primarily serves the surrounding black neighborhood.

About feeling accepted by the teachers, he said, "It was a hundred percent. They all want to help you as much as they can. Even before they knew I was in the ABC program. When they found I was in that and got to know me more, it was even more so."

I was surprised and puzzled that all three of these boys reported very little negative treatment because of their race. They may have been uncomfortable speaking about such things to a white woman, even though they knew me fairly well. Also, the Lower Merion community is an educated one, and overt expressions of prejudice are discouraged in the schools and likely in most homes. However, I suspect that the strongest reason is that these three boys form a very small sample group. Both Charles and Tyrell came to us unusually comfortable in their own skins. Both of them made friends at school quickly and widely. Both excellent athletes, they were popular at the school as well as in the ABC House.

Although Michael did not make many close friends at school, he arrived as an exceptionally outgoing fifteen-year-old and had such a cheerful temperament that this occasionally irritated his housemates. I can certainly imagine that he might just not pick up on subtle slights.

Other ABC boys, both black and Latino, have reported being annoyed when clerks in neighborhood stores follow them around as if they surely were going to be shoplifters. And I have on a couple of occasions been stunned when taking an ABC student someplace and had an adult, out of the blue, say something ugly about my being with a black teenager, apparently assuming this was my child and for some reason feeling entitled to comment negatively on this.

I am pleased that Charles, Tyrell and Michael did not feel they had been badly treated due to racism, but I don't want to convey that this was necessarily the case for every boy who comes through our program.

There's No One Here Who Looks Like Me

During this period we had an unusually large number of Latino boys in our program: Elvis, Jonathan and a third boy,
Peter (whom we'll learn about later), are all of Puerto Rican
heritage, and Anthony (whom we'll learn more about later)
and Edwin are Dominican. Lower Merion High School has a
small black population, but the ABC students are just about
the only Latinos. All of them found this an adjustment, but it
bothered them to different degrees.

Elvis said, "People [mostly students] weren't expecting
much of me because I was from New York and I'm a minority.
They thought I didn't really have much to add to an honors
class. People whose eyes would open up if I said something
smart in class or were doing well in the class. I was pretty
good at sports. They figured I only had something to add on
the field."

We asked Elvis if these things had changed over his time
here. He said, "I think it's changed, but I really don't care."

Elvis told us that the fact there were so few Latinos at
school didn't really matter for his social life. More important
was not having money. He said, "That and not being able to go
to senior parties where there'd be drinking." Drinking alcohol and attending parties where it is served is strictly against
our program's rules. Elvis said he didn't have much of a relationship with anybody from the high school outside of school.
Elvis, big and athletic, excelled at several sports: football, basketball and track. Although many of the ABC students make
friends through playing sports, Elvis said even that did not
provide him with friends outside of the ABC House. On the
other hand, he told us he hadn't felt especially integrated in
school in Brooklyn, either.

Edwin, a street-savvy Dominican, had a different initial
experience than Elvis did. When he came for his interview he
did not stay overnight, and he didn't spend a day at school, so

he was surprised when he arrived in the fall to discover how few Latinos there were at Lower Merion. "I thought, Whoa! It's ridiculous. Me and Anthony are the only Dominicans. There are less than ten Latinos at the school . . . If Anthony hadn't been here, I'd be alone."

Edwin claimed, nonetheless, that it was cool to be Latino at Lower Merion. He said that since the Dominican Republic is "coming up" as a tourist destination, a lot of kids have been there on vacation. "People at school are curious about my culture. We're Caribbean Latino. So how does that work, they want to know. 'So how'd your family get here?'" He added, "There's always a thing about Latino people being real romantic. Anthony [also Dominican, with striking good looks] and me happen to be one of those romantic people. It's cool . . . Girls like Latinos because we're not black; we're not white; we're in the middle. We're caramel!"

I suspect that an additional reason for their popularity stemmed from one of their cultural habits. Anthony, Jonathan and especially Edwin regularly greet friends, especially girls, with hugs. They extend this warm gesture to women whom they like. When Jonathan left—he was the youngest of this group—I suddenly realized that my seemingly endless supply of hugs from handsome teenagers had run out.

Just as Charles was conscious of being asked to give the black point of view in class, Edwin felt uncomfortable when in a history class his teacher twice asked, "How's that in New York?" or "How's that in your community?" Edwin said, "It wasn't a straightforward question about being a minority, but nobody else could relate to it. They'd just look at you . . . That's what's so good about the house. Everybody understands. I would tell the kids, 'Yo, can you believe what this big cat, this teacher, asked me at school!' And we'd start laughing and say, what an idiot!"

I commented that it sounded like his teacher was trying to bring up Edwin's urban, Latino culture but didn't know how to do it. He agreed. I asked Edwin about one of the Spanish teachers who is from Uruguay, and whom the ABC boys like a lot. I knew that she often asked Latino students to talk about their culture. Edwin said, "Mrs. Nemoy does it in a welcoming way."

When I asked him about another Spanish teacher with whom Anthony had a difficult relationship. Edwin said, "She's Americanized. She's married to a white guy." It was clear she was not Edwin's favorite person, but he went on to say, "She's just a really good teacher."

Then we talked about what other kids might say in class. "In my math class a guy who is a really good friend would say stuff like, 'They make tacos where he's from.' I always came back at him. The kids would laugh. And there'd be a riot and the teacher would get mad at us. The kid would always say, 'Let me know if it bothers you.' But if someone did it in a disrespectful manner, the whole class would support you instead of them. They'd say, 'What the hell's wrong with you! Don't talk to Edwin like that.' A lot of times you have to defend yourself. But other people defend you. It's amazing, especially in this neighborhood."

Anthony reacted quite differently to one teacher's comments. One of his English teachers used to tell the students that Anthony was important to the class because he was from a different background and could bring a different perspective to discussions. "This made me feel special." I'm not sure if the difference in his reaction from Edwin's was due to greater tact on the part of the teacher or a difference in the two boys' personalities.

Jonathan, who had spent much of his childhood in Puerto Rico, experienced an unusual incident in class stemming from his Puerto Rican heritage. One day during his junior year, his U.S. History teacher mentioned in class that Jonathan couldn't vote in the U.S. because he was Puerto Rican. A few days later Jonathan told me about it and asked if it was true. "I don't think that's right," I told him.

"Well, he must know," he answered. "He's the teacher."

I wasn't convinced, but to verify it I called our congress-man's local office. The young man who took my call told me he, too, thought Puerto Ricans had the vote, but he would re-search it for me to be sure. A few days later he called to tell me he had checked with the State Department. He affirmed that Puerto Ricans can vote in U.S. elections. Jonathan seemed re-lieved when I told him.

Later I asked Jonathan how he felt when the teacher said this. He admitted it made him feel a little uncomfortable, but said it didn't really matter because he wasn't interested in politics anyway. Since Jonathan has coped with a life chockfull of challenges with a robust ability to just move on, I can't judge whether this incident really did bother him or not. I had met his teacher several times, and feel confident his comment was not motivated by prejudice, just ignorance. But, in this case, his tossed-off comment carried an air of au-thority. After all, he was teaching Advanced Placement U.S. History.

Were You in a Gang?

However much our boys miss their home neighborhoods and the liveliness of the inner city, they are happy to leave behind worrying about gangs, and about getting safely to and from school. They arrive here and soon discover that some of their Lower Merion classmates assume that since they come from New York City, they must have been in a gang. Knowing that they are part of an academic elite for having been selected into ABC, this comes as quite a surprise. Their reactions cov-ered a broad range.

Peter, a smallish Puerto Rican boy who had a habit of pushing the envelope, and Jonathan, who felt so intimidated by gangs and bullies at home that he took a secret leave of ab-sence from sixth grade, were delighted to discover that just because they are from inner-city neighborhoods, some class-mates perceive them as tough.

Peter said, "We didn't try to intimidate anyone, but this reputation gave us sort of an invincible aura." He felt this effect mostly during his freshman year. Afterwards, people knew him as an individual, and he said most people were nice to the ABC boys.

When Jonathan told one classmate that he was from New York, the boy said, "Are you serious? Are you in a gang?"

"I didn't take offense. It was like, Wow! I just thought it was funny."

In contrast, Elvis took umbrage from other students' as-sumptions that he'd been in a gang. His big muscular build, his athletic talents, and his frequent use of urban slang prob-ably fed their misperceptions. In turn, Elvis was shocked by some of his Lower Merion classmates' use of drugs. He said, "At home it is only the bad kids who use drugs. Here, it could be geniuses doing it."

Unlike Elvis, street-savvy Edwin was amused by some of his classmates' questions. Laughing, Edwin told us, "The first thing some people ask is, [dropping his voice] 'Were you in a gang? Did you have a posse?' I say, no man! I'm just a regu-lar kid. I don't think they're intimidated by us. They might be. I try to be a nice guy." However, if someone from the high school acted confrontational, "We'd say we're from New York. They understand that we've been through a lot of stuff and don't mess with us."

Tyrell, who came to us from a happy family in Brooklyn, has a scar on his shoulder that he got playing football. Sev-eral times in gym another student, knowing where he came from, asked if he got that in a knife fight. He'd tell them no and explain how he got it. At other times a classmate would ask if everyone in Brooklyn carries guns. Tyrell told them, "Not everyone. I didn't." He told me, "Instead of my ridiculing them for it, I'd just try to inform them." He said a lot of kids from Lower Merion have never been to New York City. They see movies, they hear rap music and think it's all like that.

He acknowledged that some of his housemates were bothered by these questions, but said his attitude was that the students asking were just ignorant. And curious. He responded by simply answering their questions.

You Are Always on My Back

I co-chaired the board's academic committee for many years, and worked closely with the staff tutors. My partner, Mary Storey, was a retired teacher in Lower Merion's challenge program. She had also been a guidance counselor in the school system and was a terrific resource.

How many evenings did Mary and I spend in the ABC House's stuffy staff office along with one of the house tutors, talking with one boy after the other about his report card or report from school conferences? We would start with any boys who were having serious trouble in a class, move on to those with any C's and, if there were time, call in boys who were making all A's and B's to congratulate them. I remember well the seesaw we often balanced on—praising good grades and effort, and trying to encourage and shore up flagging spirits when boys were struggling in one class or several. When we cajoled and prodded boys to try harder, and gave suggestions about using school and tutor resources, we tried not to sound scolding, but I suspect we didn't always succeed.

Many boys have told me how they hated to be brought into the house office for these talks. One evening when we were meeting with the boys, my daughter, who was home from college on break, came with me and spent the evening tutoring. On the way home, she told me about boys groaning when they were called in to meet with us, and other boys teasing them saying, "Dude, you're in trouble!" Hoping to appear less ogre-like, Mary often brought along donuts and I, home baked brownies, but we knew it didn't fully work.

Students selected for A Better Chance programs are an elite, chosen for academic promise. Most of them come from less academically demanding schools where they often have made very good grades without doing much homework. At Lower Merion, they are confronted with high expectations and a lot of homework, especially in honors classes, and are with classmates who have almost all been in this excellent school system since elementary school. Many of our boys are shocked by this when they arrive. In addition, most arrive with some lacks in knowledge or skill levels. This is most apparent in math, but sometimes in English classes as well.

When I asked Elvis about challenges he faced, he said, "There were some gaps because I was starting at a different point going into high school than a lot of my peers were. With enough effort every year, my grades have gone up. I did bad in biology my freshman year. [Elvis's idea of bad was not really bad.] A few of the kids in the class, their parents either taught bio in different schools or, like three of them had doctors as parents. I expected challenges every year. I got it in some areas more than others."

As freshmen, ABC boys have to adjust to these harder expectations and workload at the same time they are missing home, living in a group house and dealing with so many differences in their new environment. In addition, many have only sketchy study and organizational skills. One of the staff tutors' most important jobs is to help them with this. I remember being at the house one evening during study hall when a tutor sat on the living room floor making Peter, a freshman then, take everything out of his stuffed backpack and then helping him organize all of his assignments, exams and other school papers into groups. Piles of his papers covered the whole length of the living room.

For the boys, ways of dealing with academic challenges included working very hard (Elvis, Michael and Jonathan come readily to mind), deciding C's are okay, or giving up on a course or two. The latter category of boys were the ones who consumed the most energy from Mary and me—trying to motivate them, encouraging them to meet with their teachers, and to use the house tutors more often. Often this helped, but unfortunately sometimes it did not.

By their second year in the program, most boys found a way of meeting the demands in their classes. While we normally schedule freshman into only a few honors classes, if they are doing well, they move up to more honors classes, so sophomore year usually brings on more work. By sophomore year they are required to maintain a grade point average of 2.8, so the pressure never really goes away. Students who consistently don't manage to maintain that minimum GPA are often dismissed from the program after their sophomore year. During the seven years of events in this book, three boys were dismissed for consistently poor grades. Charles's opinion of how that could happen was, "you have to not be really applying yourself." He thought they were smart kids, but just not mature enough. He mentioned one boy who "just wasn't doing anything, like he forgot he was here to go to school."

With all the challenges that the boys faced, I am struck by one fact. When I looked over a collection of old report cards for the boys in this book, I usually saw this message at the bottom: CONGRATULATIONS. YOU HAVE MADE THE HONOR ROLL.

Where to Sit at Lunch

Any kid new to a school faces a challenge in the cafeteria at lunchtime on where to sit. How each ABC student dealt with this could be a metaphor for how he connected at Lower Merion High School.

Most of the African American students at the high school self-segregated at lunch by sitting at an all-black table. Some also gravitated to benches in a first floor lobby at lunchtime and during free periods during their day. For years this bothered me. Did the other students shun them, I wondered, or were they for some reason just more comfortable sitting together? Reading Beverly Daniel Tatum's book, *Why Are All the Black Kids Sitting Together in the Cafeteria?* was a revelation. Tatum, a psychologist and president of a black college, argues that at an age when teenagers are figuring out issues of identity, black students who are minorities in their high schools can derive great comfort from sitting and talking with others who share their racial identity.

This would make it understandable for the African American ABC students to choose to sit at the black table. But what of our Hispanic students, some of whom, such as Elvis, are fairly light skinned?

While our ABC students eat breakfast together in the cafeteria, with three different lunch periods, deciding where to sit is more complicated. Michael claimed that it depends on the ABC student whether or not he sits at the "black table." The choices are complicated because our students are usually enrolled in a mixture of honors and standard college prep classes. Because our boys are often the only non-Asian students of color in their honors classes, if they make friends in those classes, those students are likely to be white.

Michael made his own way in the lunchroom. For the first six weeks Michael didn't know anyone to sit with, so he ate by himself. None of the other ABC boys had that lunch period. Michael said, "I always sat in the same place. It only took five or ten minutes to eat. Then I'd do homework." Michael, in spite of his excellent social skills, felt quite lonesome. One day a girl he knew because he was managing the freshman basketball team saw him and invited him to eat with her and her friends. When he told us this story three years later, his voice still registered gratitude. During his senior year he regularly ate with four other ABC students, two juniors and two freshmen, because they all had the same lunch period. Apparently, he did not branch out much to connect with other classmates, but preferred the comfort of eating with his housemates.

Elvis got into a jam his freshman year when he broke up with a girl he was dating at school. When he breaks up, he chooses to be dramatic about it, and he refused to speak to her. Since this girl still sat at the black table, he felt he could no longer sit there and had to find another place to eat.

Elvis told us that he usually sat by himself. He knew people he sat next to in classes, but he didn't consider any of those people his friends. Even though he was on several sports teams, which is a common way for the ABC students to make friends, he said he didn't have much of a relationship with classmates who were not ABC students.

Charles also started off eating at the black table when he first came to ABC in tenth grade, but did so less often the next two years he was here. He said everybody at the ABC House followed this pattern to some degree: the younger kids were apt to sit there, but many eventually moved on to sitting with white friends at least some of the time. Charles, a gentle-mannered boy, exuded a comfortable presence in the world. He slid into place in the ABC House, and I would guess at the high school as well. When he came for his interview as a prospective student, he spent a day at the high school shadowing one of the ABC students. Board member Marjorie Merklin reported that while she stood with him on the train platform in Ardmore waiting for the train that would take him home to New York, a couple of teenaged girls who were standing on the opposite platform spied him, and hollered out, "Are you coming to Lower Merion next year? We hope so."

Tyrell, whose father had accompanied him on his first visit to Ardmore, also had an easy transition to being at Lower Merion. He sat with whatever ABC students had the same lunch period for the first few days. After a week he'd had time to get to know other people, so he started, "branching out. I wouldn't sit in one place for a whole period. I'd get my lunch, eat in one spot, then I'd go over here and play cards, or go another place and do something else. I made my rounds. I'd be over here with my black friends, then I'd be over there with my athlete friends, then over with my nerdy friends, or with girls. I was all over the place."

He thought one reason he had so many friends was because he didn't stay with just one group. At Lower Merion he was around a bigger variety of people than he would have met at home in Brooklyn. Tyrell had always struck me as a good-natured boy, but even so, I was surprised at how socially connected he must have become shortly after he arrived.

When Edwin arrived, ABC student Sam (not his real name), then a senior, introduced him to his friends at the black table. It must have been a perfect match. Sam, a very outgoing boy, had lots of friends, and Edwin, a great dancer who seems to glide through life with Latino music playing in his head, is one of the most sociable people I have ever met. However, late in his senior year Edwin, who is Dominican, was still sitting almost exclusively at the black table. He told me that he was more comfortable there. Those were the people who were more familiar to him. His middle school in New York was mostly Dominican. His girlfriend during his senior year was Caucasian, a very pretty, blonde fellow cheerleader, but he still seemed to feel uncomfortable sitting at a white table.

Edwin's behavior surprised me. Voted by his classmates his senior year as "most charming," he seemed to be well liked by everybody. When he gave his presentation for his senior project, a dozen classmates showed up to hear him. Why then should he have felt uncomfortable sitting anywhere but at the black table? His warm, huggy ways masked a boy who was quite sensitive and emotional. Of all the boys, he was the most prone to tears. Because the whole world appeared to like him, did we miss that he was less comfortable here then we thought? Did we miss an opportunity to help him with this?

Hanging on to an Identity

Afro Love and Do-rags

In the run-up to the second annual poetry night event, Eric, then a shy freshman, struggled to come up with a topic, let alone a poem. Told that it was a house requirement that he write and read one, he said he couldn't do it. At some point the other boys started throwing out suggestions and words for him to use. Jay thinks it was Elvis who suggested the title. Finally, Eric sat and wrote his poem. A few nights later he stood, a six-foot-three fourteen-year-old, shifting his weight uneasily before the assembled adults, and read:

Afro Love
Walking down the hallway with my nappy hair,
All the people look and stare.
Each strand of hair like a stick,
People shouting, "Bro where's ur pick?"
You ask why I can't get no girls—
Take a look at my jeri curls
Because I refused to get my head shaved
My hair raises and shoots
That's cause I'm going back to my nappy roots.

When the audience convulsed with laughter, Eric fled. Jay coaxed him back to accept his prize for the most humorous poem, telling him over and over that we were laughing over his poem, not at him. However, when the staff told the boys to write a brief essay and read it before the board the following fall, Eric adamantly refused, still not convinced he hadn't been the target of the laughter. Nevertheless, by the next April at poetry night he stood before us, a bit more at ease, and read the sequel:

Afro Love Part 2: Ghetto Suga Project Stories

Cut my hair & grew it back
People, rise up off my back!
Got it done, no money paid.
Look at me, man, I got braids!
Singing all the project songs,
Who knew nappy could go to right from wrong?
Designer braids on my head
Can't even go to bed
Once a trend, now it's not
Some people with braids is a not.
Songs of the projects, we sing.
"Jay, do I really look like Don King?"

While worrying about one's hair and trying out different styles is a common preoccupation among teenagers, for many of the ABC boys the issue has a particular twist. Their hair is often of a different texture than that of most of their classmates, and styles popular on the streets of their home areas are quite different from those worn in Lower Merion. What to do? Most of our boys quite consciously hang on to ethnic urban styles.

For his first two years with us, Tyrell wore his hair close-cropped; but during his junior year, he and Charles, then a senior, shaved their heads just for basketball season, startling us all the first time they did it. The next year when he was a senior, Tyrell wore braids. He informed me it would last about two weeks and would be itchy by the end because he couldn't really wash his hair.

Elvis, a well-built and talented athlete, periodically shaved his head, particularly during basketball and track season.

Other times he wore a haircut similar to what many of his Lower Merion classmates wore, or had it close cropped.

Anthony, with his striking Dominican good looks, has satin-textured, thick, black curls, lush enough that he could have rented out his head for shampoo commercials. He usually took full advantage of this gift by wearing his hair full and even sometimes a bit long. Once in a while he would get his hair cut quite short and insist that I comment on it. I think Anthony used his allowance to patronize a barber—more than once he was late for appointments with me because he was at the barbershop.

Edwin, whose hair is tightly curled, often wore braids. The do-rags he used to make the braids tidy became a signature accessory after one of the cheerleading coaches told him he should always wear one when he was performing. Thus, an accessory that is usually worn informally at home, became something he frequently wore in other places.

Edwin, like many of the ABC students, was very conscious of being clean and "looking right." One day when he was a senior, I overheard him chiding a freshman who was sporting a sloppily done set of braids, perhaps the boy's first. "Dude, go put on a do-rag."

Language and Accents

Tyrell told me that his suburban classmates knew he was from the inner city just from his accent. His accent was different from that of black students who lived in Ardmore, he added.

While Elvis regularly dressed in the loose-fitting urban style, his style of speech was probably the most striking sign of his urban roots. He wrote Standard English for school assignments and was devoted to writing poetry, but his speech was full of shrugs, slang and "yeahs." I remember a flurry of adults' concern when he was a senior facing interviews at selective colleges. A couple of board members coached him in practice interview sessions. This was not necessary for his ABC pal, Michael, who spoke carefully, and clearly articulated his words.

While most of the ABC students have accents different from those of their suburban classmates, the issue of language is most pronounced for Latino students whose mother tongue is Spanish. Elvis grew up speaking English and knew little Spanish before he took it at school, but Spanish was the first language for Anthony, Edwin and Jonathan. Hanging onto their Spanish roots was very important to each of them.

Edwin explained that his dress and how he talks is his identity, "Everybody has something to say about how I talk. They say, 'Oh, you have an accent. You talk fast. You talk like a New Yorker.' That identifies me." But Spanish itself is essential to Edwin's identity. He said, "I can't maintain my culture without Spanish." Edwin and Jonathan took honors and AP Spanish at Lower Merion.

Anthony said he didn't have any problem hanging onto his Dominican identity. He attributed this to two things: his Spanish language and the fact that he was two years older than most boys when he first came to ABC. He was already a sophomore when he applied, and he agreed, reluctantly, to repeat his sophomore year in order to get into our program. Being older made him more confident of his own identity. (He was also confident of his artistic talent: Anthony's application package included a self-portrait sketch, and at the orientation put on by the National ABC for all beginning ABC scholars, he quickly became known as "the Artist.")

Anthony added that being able to speak Spanish in the house, especially with Edwin, who speaks the same dialect, made it easier to keep this important connection. He didn't think that the way he talked had changed much from being at Lower Merion. "One of the things I love about myself is my language. My language is my culture." Anthony also felt that he would always fit in at home. He thought that boys who came when they were younger might find this harder.

Anthony described what happened sometimes when he and Edwin were speaking Spanish in front of a staff member. "I think it is very unfair when you are speaking your native language and they say, don't speak your language around me. Speak English. And I ask them why and they say, you may be saying things about me. And I tell them, 'The thing is if you were minding your own business you wouldn't have to worry about us speaking our language or speaking about you.'"

Baggy Pants and Oversized Shirts

Dress is another way that the boys hang onto their inner-city identities. Tyrell described this dress as "baggy jeans, oversized tee shirts and Timberland boots." He told me he didn't want to start dressing like kids at Lower Merion do. When I asked him whether, if he were at Lower Merion but just living with a family, not with other boys at the house, he would change the way he dressed, he said, "No. I'm a real confident guy."

Elvis regularly dressed in exactly the style that Tyrell described. However, Tyrell identified Michael as always the different one in the house in terms of dress: Michael wore Abercrombie and Fitch clothes, he said, while most of the boys just wore "regular" clothes. However, Michael insisted to me that he never wore Abercrombie and Fitch clothes. Michael's background was more middle-class than most of the boys', and his more conventional style of dress reflected that. I also never saw him in braids or with a shaved head.

Anthony, who had very little money, was shocked by some Lower Merion students' dress when he first got to Ardmore.

He said he thought everybody would be dressed in the latest fashions, ". . . like Nikes and hundred dollar jeans, but some wore like pajama pants. There was this kid who had sneakers so broken down that he just taped them." To an untrained eye, the oversized clothes that most of the ABC boys wear might appear sloppy, but many of the boys were very conscious of having clean clothes and "looking right."

Clothes were another way that Edwin consciously hung on to his urban roots. About his Lower Merion classmates, Edwin said, "The boys," dropping his voice low, "they wear tight pants."

Asked if he'd be uncomfortable dressing that way, he said, "I'd never dress like that!" He told us that a few white students try to ape inner-city dress but he and his ABC housemates think they are silly. He thinks they're white people trying to dress like black people. He thinks they are trying to copy what they see on TV, not copying the ABC students.

In *Blacks in the White Elite*, a book about the first cohort of ABC students, most of them placed in private prep schools, the authors recount a story about dress. One student's advisor took one look at his "ghetto," housing-project clothes and took him shopping for blue blazers, gray flannel slacks, suits and proper black shoes, giving the clear message: this was the dress suitable, even required, for the life the student was moving into.

I have no idea whether some private schools still require ABC students to conform to a uniform style of dress, but I am glad that we do not. Our students spend their teen years straddled between two cultures. They move back and forth between school in Lower Merion, and holidays and summers at home. Keeping their dress may be one way they hold on to a constant sense of identity in the midst of all the adjustments they have to make to be here. They are not required to dress for a role they may not, at least initially, feel they fit into.

Tyrell stated the point eloquently when he said, "The way I dress is just me."

The Struggles

Culture, race and ethnic differences are not the only challenges the ABC boys face coming to Lower Merion.

Tyrell told me, "When Charles and I were walking around Ardmore, going to Bella Italia or something like that, if we saw a Bentley"—and he reached his long arm across the table and swept his middle finger down—"we'd go over and touch it." He dotted an imaginary car and continued, "That was the closest we'd ever been to a Bentley."

Tyrell added, "I remember freshman year there was a kid in our class. We were talking at lunch and some kids said, his parents are rich. One day his dad went out for a walk, just went for a walk, and came back with a Jaguar. Stopped by the Jaguar dealership, bought a car and drove it home! It was stuff like that, seeing these Jaguars and Bimmers and Benzes and Bentleys."

Our students attend a high school whose parking lot is awash in cars: some belonging to students, some lent to classmates by their parents. The student newspaper perennially prints petitions to allocate more parking spaces for students' cars. Most of the ABC boys share their classmates' intense interest in cars, but access is only a distant wish. Furthermore, our policy forbids ABC students from even driving someone else's car while they are in the program because of our concern about liability. But they are normal American male teenagers, and most of them can reel off names and characteristics of a long menu of cars, especially expensive ones.

Not having access to cars is one way that the boys feel the effects of being poor or relatively poor while attending school in such an affluent community. Not all their classmates are from upper-middle-class or upper-class families, but many are, and that's what the boys tend to notice. What helps, and helps a lot, is to come home to the ABC House where the guys who they live with understand how this feels.

The four live-in staff members are usually young adults recently graduated from college. Some don't own cars, and those who do have modest ones. Jay got his first car the summer before his second year at ABC when his older brother gave him a used Jeep. Jay loved to drive the boys to school events, to outside classes or doctor's appointments. The boys quickly dubbed his car the Jaymobile.

Jay remembers hearing the boys talk about "the struggles." Tyrell told me, "I'm confident to say that would be something talked about in the house since it started. Most kids who come here are from underprivileged families. Everyone talks about the Black struggle, the Hispanic struggle. It's not specific to the house. We talk about it in our family."

Elvis, who had grown up poor in Brooklyn, helping his dad with his hot dog stand, explained that he found the economic differences with his classmates much harder to deal with than being a student of color. He said, "The struggle is talked about a lot in our culture."

Another way that the boys feel different from their classmates is school vacations. Tyrell said that after spring break, "Different kids would come back with tans. 'Where'd you go?' [Someone would ask.] 'Oh, Brazil,' or Cancun. Or they'd go skiing. In class they would ask, 'What did you do? Where'd you go?' And I would say 'I went from my bedroom to the bathroom, to the kitchen, back to my bedroom. I vacationed in Brooklyn.'"

While living in the ABC House provides a buffer against the discomfort of attending school with so many affluent classmates, within the house tensions over money or the lack of it sometimes bubble to the surface.

The year after Tyrell graduated, the general conversations about "the struggles" in the house turned into something else.

Jay remembers it as being like a private joke. Boys would say, "Jay, you just don't understand what the struggles are." Elvis and Anthony in particular were focused on this. In the midst of this, Michael, whose background set him slightly apart on this matter, wrote a poem as a kind of parody on this ongoing subject that he called "The Struggle." A few stanzas show the theme.

> Some people say, the struggle brings us down
> But I will use the struggle to get out of this town
> It will empower me to live on,
> And to raise myself above this hated town . . .
>
> They may blame it on the man for bringing them down
> Nah, nah, they bring themselves down
> By doing nothing about the struggle . . .
>
> For me, it started with my first breath of fresh air
> The environment I was put into,
> And the people I was surrounded by
> Were the struggle . . .
> I used that to empower me, and do something with my life
> Looked at my roots and saw where I came from, and said
> Yes, I survived . . .

I asked some of the guys to help me understand this issue, and Elvis said, "It was sort of a joke on Michael. The whole thing was about me arguing with Michael about who had a rougher life. He has a Visa bucks [debit] card. No kid in the struggles has a Visa bucks card. Anthony made up the name Silver Spoon Michael."

He continued, "Michael has Michael Jordan sneakers."

Anthony added, "A new pair every month."

"Naw, naw," Michael protested.

After Michael wrote the poem, the teasing had escalated. Now laughing, Elvis said, "I was pretty mad. We used to have serious arguments on chore night. We'd yell at each other like who has a bigger hole in his sock."

Michael added, "Who has a hole in his underwear."

"Who eats spam, who had more Kool-Aid in their life? Who drank from the fire hydrant?"

Michael admitted that when he wrote the poem, he didn't realize he was the butt of the joke about the struggles. He added about the arguments, "The contest is who can out-poor each other."

"Michael doesn't really need ABC. He's had all those trips out of the country. He's flown on a plane," Elvis said.

"But I went to Canada for a family reunion, to Guyana with my father to visit family."

"And then there was the cruise."

"We went on a day cruise to the Bahamas. It only cost a hundred dollars." His mother and stepfather had moved to Florida the summer before his junior year, and now lived in an apartment there, a safer and more comfortable place than the neighborhood in Brooklyn where Michael grew up.

Michael continued, "Once in a while Elvis will claim I have a yacht in my backyard. We have a lake in our backyard at the apartment house. I showed him a picture."

"He lives in a complex," Elvis said, his voice a sneer, "With a swimming pool! And alligators."

"Snakes and ducks."

Whatever the tensions within the house, the boys are united in their interest in cars. Each ABC boy is assigned a host family whom they visit monthly. One of Tyrell's best memories of Sunday afternoons with his host family is when his host father, Rob McCord, would take him for a ride in his silver Porsche with the top down. Usually just the two of them would ride around the Main Line, but sometimes Rob would tuck his two young sons into the tiny backseat. Then all the guys would tool around, the breeze kissing their cheeks, bonding in that swell car.

Street Spanish

Over the years that I've worked with the ABC program, I have had the opportunity to interact with many of the high school's teachers about one or another of our boys. My general impression is that most of the teachers are quite pleased to have the ABC boys in their classes and usually regard them as agreeable, respectful young men. I have often sensed that some teachers particularly like working with our boys because they are not from the comfortable backgrounds shared by many students at the school. Our boys have commented that most of their teachers are very helpful and nice to them.

When Anthony, one of our Dominican students, arrived to start with us as a sophomore, I signed on to be his academic advisor. At the high school's open house that fall, I went up after each teacher's talk and introduced myself. I told them that Anthony was an ABC student and that I would be following his academic progress. The responses I got were quite gracious—until I got to his third-year honors Spanish class.

Since Spanish is Anthony's native language, I was expecting he would stand out in the class, and I anticipated the same warm reception that the other teachers had given me. Instead, his teacher stunned me by saying, "That boy needs to work harder. He thinks he knows everything. He knows street Spanish!"

Street Spanish! How I have come to hate that phrase. Over the years that Mary Storey, a fellow board member, and I supervised the ABC academic program, most of our Latino students told us at some point, "My teacher says I just know street Spanish." Many of the boys struggled in Spanish classes far more than we thought they should.

We both found it hard to sort out what was going on. Neither Mary nor I know Spanish, so we could not independently assess their skills. Our boys arrive with a wide variation of language exposure. For many, Spanish is the principal language spoken at home, for others, not. But that variation seems to have had little effect on some teachers' perception that they only know street Spanish. Was it a difference in accent or the Spanish of their parents' home country? Was it social class?

Many, although not all, of our boys struggled in the honors Spanish classes. Some dropped Spanish after the third-year course or moved down from honors level to a standard class. Others switched to another language after second year Spanish. For a while, ABC was helping to fill up the school's Latin classes as boys transferred to Latin.

Knowing this history did little to help me understand what was going on with Anthony, nor what to do about it. He had lived in the Dominican Republic until he was five years old. Spanish was his first and only language until he moved to the United States. He was enrolled in bilingual classes through fifth grade, and Spanish is the language spoken in his home. I had thought this class would be a breeze for him.

Three times a year, the high school holds scheduled, individual conferences with teachers for parents whose children are having trouble in a class. In the ABC program, we schedule conferences for each academic advisor with as many of their student's teachers as possible, regardless of how the student is doing in a class. Each advisor takes his or her student along so they both hear the report on where any weaknesses lie, and the teacher's advice for improvement.

At the first set of parent-teacher conferences, Anthony and I had pleasant and helpful meetings with his history, English and physics teachers. Then we got to the meeting with his Spanish teacher. Would she have softened from my last meeting with her? No. She said directly to Anthony, "You need to work harder. You think you know more than you do." She went on to tell him that he needed to study grammar more as he had gaps in written grammar and that the class was going to get harder. Probably all good advice for him, but what sticks in my memory, as it stuck in my craw at the time, was the aggressive anger she seemed to be directing towards him. Anthony handled it with poise, but I could tell he was surprised.

I took him out for a snack afterwards so we could talk. While I enjoyed watching him wolf down a large sandwich and side of fries, I told him, "Anthony, you need to figure out how to get along with that teacher." He knitted his dark, dramatic eyebrows and looked up at me. As we talked, he admitted that he didn't always turn his assignments in on time, something I had learned from his English teacher as well. Anthony, who was also a talented artist, did tend to be late around the house, too—something I came to ascribe to his dreamy, artistic temperament.

This was a no-brainer, I told him: he should just hand in his assignments on time. Always. Then he admitted he had gotten off to a bad start with his Spanish teacher when he corrected her use of a word. I laughed and told him that was another no-brainer. Don't do it again. Ever. He told me he had already figured that out.

He pulled a B in his first report card, to my great relief. But the next teacher conference was more or less a repeat of the first one. She warned Anthony that the literature they were reading would get harder. He had the vocabulary to do well, but needed to work on grammar. "You think you know it, but you don't." She told him he was lazy. After we left her room, I started rubbing Anthony's back to comfort him—or maybe to calm myself. Why did I feel as if the two of us would soon be summoned to the principal's office? Once again Anthony got a B in the class, although I hoped he could reach an A the next time.

By the third conference in the spring, the teacher was a bit mellower. She complimented him on taking part in class discussions. Still, I detected little warmth expressed toward a boy who loves his native language and speaks it with seeming fluency and exuberance.

When it came time to select classes for the coming year, Anthony adamantly refused to take fourth-year Spanish. "I don't need it," he kept saying. "It's time to move on to another language." Months later, when I thought Anthony had had time to gain perspective on what had gone on in his Spanish class, I talked to him about it.

Speaking of his first impression of the class he said, "I was so surprised that some of the students could write Spanish so well and could speak it so well. I could speak it. I just didn't know how to write it as well as the other kids in the class."

Anthony told me that fairly early in the term the teacher, in front of the whole class, told him he spoke street Spanish. I asked him how that felt. "It was one of those things you say one minute and then forget about the next."

"The teacher or the class?" I asked.

"Both. But I remembered."

He went on to say, "It made me want to work harder and outshine everybody. I always participated in class a lot. Eventually students started to say, 'Oh, he speaks fluently. He speaks real fast.'"

"How long did it take before you felt comfortable in class?"

"December."

A bit later he commented, "How can this be street Spanish when it is the Spanish I speak at home? It's the Spanish my whole country speaks. How can she say my whole country speaks street Spanish?"

Anthony went on to say, "I was disappointed at first. I think of language as what is spoken at a specific location. I realize I need proper Spanish at some places, like to communicate to a businessperson. If I keep my regular Spanish I can communicate with my culture. I feel like I need both, but mostly the language I speak at home."

At the end of his junior year Anthony took the SAT II in Spanish. I hoped he would do well on it, but because of what his teacher had said about his grammar skills, I worried. Apparently, he was worried as well. His spoken fluency would not help him much on this paper and pencil test. And it had been a whole year since he'd taken a Spanish class. In midsummer I heard what his score was: out of a possible 800, Anthony had scored 770. Some street Spanish!

CHAPTER 4

Bonding

Our ABC students arrive as young teenagers to live in a houseful of strangers: adult staff and the other students in the program. What happens after that forms the core of what makes the ABC Community School Programs distinctive and special.

Among the Boys

Buddies I

Mutt and Jeff. That's the tag that people put on Charles and Tyrell when they first started hanging out together. Charles arrived at our program as a broad-shouldered six-foot-three, athletically slender sixteen-year-old. Tyrell, outgoing from the start, was a skinny fourteen-year-old, still only five-four or five—just starting the growth spurt that would eventually shoot him well past six feet. The fall they arrived, they were joined by another freshman who Tyrell already knew because they had attended the same middle school in Brooklyn. However, that boy bailed out after only a few weeks, a victim, it seemed, of terminal homesickness. That left Charles and Tyrell in an unusual situation.

Because we had not taken any new students the previous year, Charles was the only sophomore, and, with the other new student gone, that left Tyrell as the only freshman. Charles told me, "Everybody had been here for at least two years. We were really new to this and everybody else was just about old to it. We even came on our visit together." Charles didn't look on Tyrell as a younger brother. "We were kind of like in it together."

About the older ABC students Charles said, "When I was coming in, the older guys were like big brotherly to us." However, most of the older boys enjoyed active social lives outside the house, while at first Charles and Tyrell did not. Because they hung around the house more than the other boys did, they started to think of it as their house. "Even senior year, I was definitely a presence in the house. It was our house."

Early on, they took to playing ping-pong in the basement, and soon they were playing almost daily. They also shot baskets at the net in the backyard and, when basketball season came, they both joined the team. Charles thinks they really bonded over that, and basketball became a central passion in both of their lives.

Charles had been active in his mother's Pentecostal Christian church, and remained quite religious. Tyrell told me that at first Charles would only listen to gospel music, while the other boys all liked rap. He also wouldn't dance or go to school dances. When the ABC program hosted dances at the house, Charles helped the adult chaperones. In spite of that, the other ABC students accepted Charles very well. Later, Charles loosened up and would listen to rap, and he went to his senior prom. Charles later told me that even before he came to ABC he listened to some rap, and he especially liked Notorious B.I.G.

Charles said that Tyrell was his best friend in the house. While most of his friendships at school crossed racial lines, that was one way his friendship with Tyrell was different. Another was, "We lived together. And we came from the same place." Both Charles and Tyrell had come from stable, close-knit families in difficult neighborhoods in Brooklyn. If he were upset by something at school, Charles could come home and talk to Tyrell about it, knowing that Tyrell would understand what he was feeling.

For his part, Tyrell said it was important to him that he could always talk to Charles. When I asked if this especially mattered when he was down, he replied. "I don't remember ever being down." I commented that Michael used to irritate his housemates because he never seemed to be depressed. To that Tyrell said, "I was never in a bad mood, either. Even if I was, I had someone to talk to. I had Charles."

For two years Charles and Tyrell had been a tight pair. Then Michael, with his friendly, outgoing personality, showed up as a freshman. Right from the first, Michael followed Charles around. Charles, who was now a senior, and Tyrell, a junior, looked on Michael as sort of a younger brother, and enjoyed him—most of the time. Michael was playful and liked to tease. But he had one fault: he talked too much. Way, way too much.

Tyrell told me, "Sometimes when Chaz and I just got tired of listening to him, we'd pick him up and stuff him in a room."

Charles said, "We used to lock him in the library and hold the door, not let him get out. He kept on fighting back. He wouldn't shut up.

"Michael would tease me about my younger sister. He was always telling me how cute my little sister was. Or if Tyrell had a girlfriend, he'd say he was going to flirt with her, anything to irritate us. We would chase him down. Beat him up; get him in a hammerlock. It was very playful. Like a family."

Michael, then about five-nine, would walk up to Charles, by this time a six-foot-six basketball star, barrel out his chest and bump into him. Charles would roll his eyes, puff out his cheeks, and chase him: through the living room, into the dining room, into the kitchen, the hallway, past the staircase, into the living room again. Michael was small enough that he could pivot through doorways and slide past obstacles while Charles, the program's gentle giant, thundered on his heels.

Charles said, "It was funny. He was just a skinny kid. But every time I went after him, some freak accident would happen. I'd stub my toe or bang my knee into the staircase. Every time, I'd be the one who got hurt. One time when I was chasing him, something fell off the counter in the kitchen, rolled around the door into the dining room where I was, and hit my toe."

Each spring the ABC board hosts a graduation party the weekend before the high school's graduation. The year Charles was a senior, board members, host parents, staff members, and students ate a stand-up buffet lunch and mingled. Afterward, everyone listened to an inspirational speech by the Dean of Haverford College, who was African American. Jay remembers that most, but not all, of the guests had left when Michael came up to Charles, stuck out his chest as if he were going to manhandle him, and gave him a small push. Charles rose to the challenge. They raced through the first floor rooms and soon Tyrell and another student were chasing around as well, all of them yelling. Michael banged out of the kitchen's back door and in a minute all of them were running around the back yard—comic relief after an afternoon when they had to be on company behavior.

Charles felt that his real graduation ceremony was on a different day. That night he, Tyrell and Michael went into the library, shut the door and "turned the lights off, lit candles, turned on my favorite rap song, "Juicy" by Notorious B.I.G. It was like a culmination of my time here."

Jay said that Charles, whose musical tastes had broadened beyond Gospel, particularly liked to sing along to Whitney Houston's rendition of "I Will Always Love You." The year after Charles graduated, Jay would sometimes hear Michael playing the same piece, singing along loudly, off key. Missing Charles.

Buddies II

When Elvis and Michael were newly arrived freshmen, week-end evenings were the hardest. In the quiet suburbs of Lower Merion there seemed to be nothing to do. After a few weeks they hit on walking to a Starbucks, about a half-mile from the ABC House. There they would sit, drink a cup of hot chocolate and talk. At least they were in a public place with strangers milling about.

They laughed about the anomaly of becoming friends, sort of buddies. On one thing they agreed: this would never have happened in New York. There's their different heritage—Michael being black and Elvis, Puerto Rican. And over and over, Elvis would say, "Besides, Mike is not the sort of person I would have picked out for a friend at home."

Michael was slender, perfectly proportioned with a chocolate complexion. He kept his hair close cropped. Although he saw himself as still dressing in an urban style, he wore his clothes fitting fairly close to the body. Everything about him seemed neat and self contained, even his speech. Michael spoke clearly, in well-modulated sentences.

Elvis is light-skinned enough that he was occasionally taken as one of the many Jewish students at Lower Merion High School. But his clothes and speech spoke of his inner-city origins: oversized pants and jackets, and the sardonic "yeahs" that punctuated his speech.

Although they spent a lot of their free time together throughout their four years at ABC, they both admitted that they argued quite a bit, and occasionally got into scuffles.

Michael said, "For example. I don't like things on my bed. Early in the morning and Elvis put his dirty book bag on my bed. And I said, 'Elvis! Take your book bag off my bed.' He didn't listen. We just got into it."

Michael continued, "I don't like people touching me on my face, and freshman year he touched me on my face so I touched him on his face and he got really mad. Then we were in each other's faces for a while."

To this Elvis said, "You just like to get me mad."

I thought they were exaggerating their conflicts, especially since they hung out together so much. They both claimed they would eventually invite each other to their weddings.

One weekend evening in the spring of their freshman year, Elvis and Michael headed out together as usual. That weekend Jay was on duty, his least favorite responsibility as a staff member. This particular evening he was working at a computer, fretting. He was now in the worst phase of weekend duty: the evening hours before curfew, and he had begun to worry. Would any of the guys not make it? Were any of them riding with classmates who were inexperienced drivers? The ABC boys are not allowed to drive, but they can and do go places with friends who drive. Would they end up at parties that had alcohol?

Board and staff members drum into the boys' heads that if that happens, they are to call immediately for a ride. If one of them called, Jay would need to track down a board member to come rescue him. This need rarely arose, but Jay had heard that teen parties at Lower Merion were often awash in alcohol.

He thought, no wonder people said raising teenagers is hard. But parents of teenagers were middle-aged, and usually had only one or two kids to worry about. He was twenty-three, and this night he was solely responsible for eight teenaged boys.

Added to these distractions was the constant ringing of the phone: boys checking in to tell him where they had decided to go next, classmates calling for boys in the house, and on and on.

He wasn't especially worried about Charles, a senior, and Tyrell, a junior. The two of them, still inseparable friends, were levelheaded and practically never missed curfew. The sophomores worried him more. Two freshmen, Michael and Elvis, had said they were walking to Bella Italia, a pizza shop on Lancaster Avenue in Ardmore, maybe a half mile away. They were both sensible boys.

Just before curfew, he heard the front door open and Michael and Elvis strode into the computer room. "Jay, there is someone at the door for you," Michael announced.

When Jay didn't immediately jump up, Elvis said, "Jay, we said there is someone at the door for you!"

While Jay walked to the front door, both boys stood far back in the hallway, watching, snickering. Jay opened the front door to see a Lower Merion police officer. My God! What happened, he thought.

"Can I help you, officer?" he asked, trying to stay the quaver in his voice.

"Everything is okay," the officer said. "I just gave these boys a ride home."

The policeman asked for Jay's name and wrote it down. After chatting for a bit and reassuring him that everything was all right, the officer finally left. Jay whirled around to face Michael and Elvis, who were still hanging back in the hallway. "What happened?" he exploded.

"We were just walking through the parking lot of Manhattan Bagel by a cop car," Michael said.

Elvis joined in, "The cop fingered us over."

The two boys described what happened next. The policeman asked where they were coming from. When they answered, Bella Italia, he said, "Oh really!" and stepped out of the car. "They've just been robbed. You," he said, pointing at Elvis, who was wearing a hoodie, "fit the description of one of the suspects."

The policeman called for backup and took their names. He told the boys to empty their pockets. While he was talking to them, another police car arrived. An older policeman got out and walked over to them.

"Then I did a stupid thing," Michael told Jay. He was getting hot, so he opened his jacket. The closure was Velcro and he just ripped it open. Instantly, the second cop reached for his gun. The boys were stunned but the first policeman waved his hand down, indicating, "Cool it, cool it."

Michael didn't know what to do, but Elvis, who had stood up to gang members in middle school, said, "Don't worry. Let me do all the talking. I've been to a seminar on how to interact with New York cops."

While the policemen were looking at the boys' IDs, the boys started talking to each other about the Simpsons. Elvis pulled out his Medicaid card and they started talking about that.

Eventually, the policemen decided they weren't the suspects. The first officer told the boys to get into his car so he could give them a ride home. He explained that it was police procedure to drive home any minor whom they had stopped and questioned.

Jay thought maybe the policeman wanted to verify that they lived at the ABC House, and gave that as his excuse. However, since the boys didn't question the explanation, he didn't bring it up.

"Guys, you could have given me some warning who it was before I went to the door," Jay complained. The boys smirked, but Jay couldn't be annoyed with them. He was just grateful they were all right.

Three years later when Michael and Elvis were talking to us about the incident for this book, they still sounded stunned over the cop having reached for his gun. Michael said he had been stopped by police in New York, but had never had one reach for his gun. Leaning back in his chair, Elvis said, "I thought it was cool that we got a ride in the cop car."

Buddies III

I was sitting with Wes Bradley (not his real name), another board member, in the ABC House living room one pleasant Sunday afternoon chatting with the family of a prospective student. Suddenly, we heard the front door bang open and the clumping of big-shoed feet in the hallway. Edwin, Peter and Anthony dashed into the living room, out of breath and all talking at once.

In a rush of words Edwin said, "Peter fell off his bike."

"Fell off!" Peter, the smallest of the three, retorted. "You ran into me."

"I ran into you because you cut in front of me!"

"Well I couldn't stop. My bike is horrible. It doesn't have any brakes."

At this point Wes stepped in and said, "Peter, why doesn't your bike have brakes? I thought Edwin was going to fix it."

Peter laughed. "I don't know. He hasn't done it yet." Peter held out his arm—it was striped with abrasions—then pulled up his pant leg to show off a skinned shin. "See! I really did get hurt."

Wes and I told Peter to go clean up the scrapes. Anthony had drifted off but Edwin was still around. Wes said, "Edwin, I thought you said you knew how to fix bikes."

"Yeah, well maybe. I worked in a bike shop. But I don't know about fixing brakes. Maybe I can."

"I thought you were going to fix the brakes before you boys went riding," Wes said. Then he jumped up and announced, "I think I'd better check that he really is cleaning up," and he left in search of antiseptics and bandages.

I stayed chatting with the adult guests while worrying that the drama might have put them off considering our program. I hoped the boys' high good humor would offset any negative impression.

Anthony, the tallest of the three, and Edwin, wiry but muscular, had met in New York at the summer orientation session that ABC national ran for new ABC Scholars, a month before they arrived in Ardmore. Edwin told me, "I was so happy to meet Anthony, another Dominican. My middle school was about eighty-five percent Dominican. I knew there'd be a lot of whites at Lower Merion. But I didn't think we'd be the only Dominicans."

Anthony said, "Edwin and I stood out a lot at orientation. Almost everybody knew us. I came home with two and a half pages full of girls' phone numbers."

Peter, who was from a Puerto Rican family, had been wishing for a good friend all of his freshman year. When Edwin and Anthony arrived, suddenly he had two best friends. Anthony said, "We clicked with Peter pretty quickly. He was very friendly to us." Soon the three were spending most of their free time together. Jay thought of them as the Three Amigos, but the boys themselves took the labels, Pretty Boy Crew and LLES (Latin Lovers Escort Service).

That spring, bike riding around the neighborhood together became one of their favorite activities. Not only did it give them exercise and fresh air, but it greatly extended their range around the community. Several times when I was driving one of them somewhere, he would say, "Oh, I recognize this street. I used to ride my bike along here."

While we do not allow ABC students to drive when they are with us, upperclassmen often have friends with access to cars and can go out with them. But these three were underclassmen, so the bikes, scruffy as they were, were their "wheels." One of the bikes belonged to Tim, a staff tutor, who loaned it to Anthony. The other two were broken-down bikes they found in the shed at the back of the house.

Many of the ABC students feel confined living in Ardmore. They are used to living in cities where there is more street life and where, sometimes, they can travel a wider area by taking public transit. This varies widely from one boy to another, but Edwin enjoyed a lot of street life in his Dominican neighborhood in Inwood Manhattan. Anthony spoke of being able to go to a dance club close to where his mother currently lived in Baltimore. Being able to ride their bikes around and explore the neighborhood mitigated, at least a little, their feelings of being isolated in the suburbs.

Another memorable bike adventure, which I came to think of as the "Great Getting Lost," happened the day they decided to ride a bike trail in Manayunk, a steeply hilly section of Philadelphia on the other side of the Schuylkill River from Lower Merion Township. Tim showed Anthony where it was on a map. Anthony, thinking he knew the way, didn't take the map with him. They cycled to Manayunk, about six miles from Ardmore, but couldn't find the trail. Nor could they find anybody on a stoop or on the street to ask for directions, as they used to do in their home cities.

Edwin told us, "We tried to stop cars, but they wouldn't stop. We were making hitchhike signs and all that." Finally, they saw a man walking to his car and surrounded him, begging for directions.

Anthony said, "He was this old guy in a nice car."

Edwin said, "He gave us directions, but it didn't help. They were too complicated." Eventually, they started to worry about getting home in time for study hall. Then they couldn't remember how to get home. Still, no one they could ask for directions.

After several hours of trial and error, they managed to find their way. They talked of the adventure for weeks.

The next school year they abandoned the bike excursions. The bikes had deteriorated even further, and the three boys were busy with other activities. Peter, always ready to push into unknown territory, had talked Edwin into joining him on the high school's cheerleading squad. In addition to the time they spent together at practices and games, the two continued to spend most of their free time with Anthony.

Edwin wrote the poem "Lil' Brother" out of feeling homesick his freshman year, but during his second year he wrote one titled, "To My Boys," about all of the ABC students. Of Peter he wrote:

> Peter who's been my boy from the beginning
> And I will love you 'til the end, 'til the last ABC inning.

Of Anthony he wrote:

> Anthony who came here with me, and proved that
> Dominican is a great thing to be.

Breakfast Together at School

Of his first day at Lower Merion High School, Jonathan, his almond eyes wide, said, "I was really, really nervous. I got off the bus and walked to that basement corridor that leads into the cafeteria. After I got my breakfast, Edwin came up to me and said, 'Hey, just so you know, we all eat together every single day for breakfast.' He pointed to the table where the other ABC students were sitting. It was the first sign that I felt part of the ABC boys."

While most students need to pay for their breakfasts, those qualifying for free lunch, which our boys do, qualify for a free breakfast, too. Although I could understand why breakfast that first day was so helpful to Jonathan, I was surprised when he went on to say how important it was to him throughout his four years with us.

"We always sat at the exact same table. It was round and had just the right number of chairs for all of us. It gave us a sense of solidarity. There is so much that happens on a daily basis in the house—conflicts, drama—that we feel divided at times. No one likes each other all the time. But when we got to school we were one unit, just the guys, looking out for each other starting from the moment we walked in."

I asked him if the older ABC boys sometimes sat at other tables, and he insisted they did not, that they all stayed together. He said at first it was just the ABC boys at their table, but over time people who became friends with boys in the house would sometimes join them. "When somebody from school became friends with one guy in the house, they became friends with everybody in the house—especially if they hang out at the house after school."

Jonathan mentioned Eric, the boy they used to call "number nine." One summer, a white family who had a teenaged son, moved in a few doors down from the ABC House. New to the area, Eric met the eight current ABC boys when school started, and soon was hanging out at the ABC House most afternoons after school. I remember being over at the house for dinner one evening and asking who the extra boy at the table was. Monica, the resident director then, said, "He's my ninth child."

Now Jonathan told me, "He was the ninth one at breakfast, too."

When we hire new staff, we tell them that eating dinner together as a group is an important part of their job, and we urge them to foster a family atmosphere at dinner. That structure was a conscious creation of our board. I was delighted to learn that the boys themselves had created another tradition, eating breakfast together, that gave them a sense of belonging and offered a way to ease the tensions of living in a group home.

Coming Home to the Guys

I have no idea why it took me so long—years—to understand what is probably the most important support that our program offers our boys: the presence of each other. I could have just asked, and almost anyone of them could have told me. From the many interviews that Jay and I conducted, I gradually came to understand how living with other boys who were going through the same challenges provided a unique buffer and sense of security for them.

As a program we provide housing, supervision by residential staff, and tutoring. A large active board, host families, and academic advisors ensure that the boys come into contact with many supportive adults. But support from their housemates provides something that is especially rich in the twenty-two community school programs. Each community school program houses its students together in a homelike atmosphere. All the other programs, the vast majority of ABC programs, are either in private boarding schools or independent day schools.

It is only in the community school programs, such as ours, that ABC students are with each other daily in a family-like setting. Charles, a very tall, gentle mannered boy, said he would have gone to a private prep school if he had been accepted into one, but in retrospect he was grateful that he came to us instead. He explained that when he was the only black student in a class and the teacher called on him to give the "black" point of view on an issue, ". . . it really helped to go home to a whole house full of guys who knew how that felt. Everybody experienced that. I remember going home and telling Tyrell, . . . and he'd say, 'I know what you mean.'"

Talking about living in the ABC House, Charles said, "Dinner was lively. We would talk about anything. Big issues. Good staff knew how to promote those discussions.

"When we did group things the staff planned, we always complained about it ahead of time. A lot of times it took place early on a Saturday morning, which you consider your free time. But, once we got there it was fun. The times when we were together were good."

Several boys told us that when someone from outside the house was a friend with one ABC student, they tended to be friends with everyone in the house. This especially helped

freshmen, who were coming into a new school not knowing anyone.

The boys also expressed clear feelings about what outsiders should know. Michael said, "We have always been good
about keeping things in the house. Like if I slap Elvis in the
face, people at school don't need to know that.

"I don't think we are quite a family but, even though we
fight and hate each other at times, we're here for each other.
When we really need each other, when times are tough, there's
nobody in this house who wouldn't go out of his way to help
another. Even if I didn't like that kid, I'd help him."

Tyrell confirmed that sense of responsibility, saying that
in the house the boys tease each other. Everyone gets picked
on with pranks. "That's what brothers do." But outside the
house, they feel responsible for each other. Tyrell was a senior
the year Peter came as a freshman. He said that since Peter
was so small, some kids at school hassled him. When he saw
this happening, Tyrell would pull the kid over later and tell
him to cool out. "I've never told Peter about it."

When wiry, street-wise Edwin was a freshman, a white
student called him a Spic. Edwin said he had come here as
a hothead and wanted the kid to fight him, but the boy
wouldn't. However, the boy kept saying nasty things about
Edwin. Then Elvis found out about it. He told the offending
student, "You're not touching my boy. If I find out you even
talked to him in a bad way, I'll calm you." Edwin reported,
"The guy never messed with me again."

Edwin told me if an ABC student is being pushed around
by outsiders, first some ABC boys would speak to the other
kid, "We say, this guy has seven brothers. We're from New
York. We don't play that stuff." If it continues, ". . . it turns
into something physical." Elvis and Michael, on the other
hand, claim the ABC students just don't get "beat up."

One year, Edwin made friends with an exchange student
from Mexico. This boy was living with an older couple, who

had no other teenagers in their house. The boy told Edwin he would love to live in the ABC House. Indeed, he was a frequent dinner guest, and once when his host parents were out of town, the ABC staff let him stay at the house for a whole week. Edwin commented on how hard it must be to be away from home and not have anyone like the ABC boys around. He would have felt really left out and would have wanted to go back to his zone high school in New York, in spite of the dangers, if he weren't living at the ABC House. "The guys in the house, they can be punks sometimes, but they've got that brotherly love thing going on. Every day you come back; you come back to the guys. It's good stuff. There are always problems because you live together, but then there's always support because you live together."

In the fall of 2003, we hosted a celebration of the program's thirtieth anniversary with a day of activities, a dinner, and a panel talk by four alumni. Among the alumni who came were four who graduated in 1981. After the dinner was over, these four ended up in the ABC House basement gathered around the pool table reminiscing into the wee hours of the morning. The current ABC students all clustered around "with their tongues hanging out," as described by one of the staff members.

Two years later Edwin wrote about that evening:

. . . They had come down for a simple socializing event to catch up with old friends and revisit their high school years. But, little did they know that they would have such a powerful and long lasting effect on us, the current ABCLM students.

Their presence was almost godlike. We looked up to these alumni the way a child would look up to his favorite super hero. They left us speechless with descriptions of their experiences here in the program we are now a part of. To hear their success stories after high school was inspirational to all of us. They encouraged us by letting us know that the struggles we endure here, away from our homes, families and loved ones, are worth every tear and drop of sweat we shed.

Summer Reading Program

Several years ago a student in the program, Juan (not his real name), repeatedly got caught breaking in-your-room curfew. A staff member coming down to the kitchen late at night would see a light on in the living room and find Juan, having snuck out of his first floor bedroom, curled up reading a book. That story, repeated over several years, always hit me with almost physical pain. I remembered my daughter as a teenager coming home and announcing, "I'm going to flop," which translated to mean she would sprawl out on her bed and bury herself in a fictional world until dinner time.

But Juan, a student with literary talents who graduated before the poetry writing began, apparently could not let anybody see him engrossed in a book. He was the student most committed to maintaining a "cool" image. For Juan, reading had to stay a secret vice.

While many of our boys come from musically rich backgrounds, with a few exceptions, reading for pleasure has not been a major part of their lives. The boys read many books required in their courses, but staff and board members, especially those who serve on the academic committee, struggle with how to encourage them to also read for enjoyment. Late one spring, Wes Bradley, then a member of the executive board, suggested that since our yearly fundraising goals had been exceeded we could buy the boys some books for summer reading.

He planned to buy each boy two books. He decided to give everyone a copy of John Krakauer's *Into Thin Air*, saying he thought the story's tension and drama would grip them. When they came back from summer vacation, we could hold a group discussion about the book. Wes wanted to select a second book for them all to read and tossed out a couple ideas, but I convinced him that we should let each boy pick out a paperback of his own choosing, since they owned so few books. Jay collected choices from the boys. Michael chose a book on web design—he was the Webmaster for the ABC program and was especially interested in computers. All the others selected fiction, mostly gritty, urban novels such as Donald Goines's *Daddy Cool* and *Never Die Alone*. A few weeks before the end of the term, Wes gave the boys their books.

Suddenly, some of the boys were diving into their books. The staff tutors worried about their reading during time they should have been studying for final exams. Our summer reading program was a success ahead of schedule.

The following September, just before school started, Wes and I joined the staff and all the students for an informal meeting to welcome them for the year. We arrayed ourselves in a circle in the living room. When our chat about academic expectations was finished, I announced we would now have a discussion of *Into Thin Air*, which they all had read during the summer. In a fit of poor judgment, I turned to the student closest to me on the left and said, "So, Sam (not his real name), what did you think of *Into Thin Air*?"

Sam, a strikingly handsome senior with chiseled features and close-cropped hair, slumped further into the couch, and, in a drawl, told us how he really couldn't say much about it as he had only gotten through the first three chapters because, "It was soooo boring." Why oh why, I asked myself had I started with the one student who had spent the last three years perfecting how to charm and to annoy all of the staff and many board members?

The other senior, a most conscientious student, was sitting next to Sam and now he allowed that he had not even gotten through three chapters because, "It was so boring."

As I called on each boy in turn, the number of chapters, then pages that reportedly had been read continued to shrink. Where one boy reported having read only two chapters, the next said he had not even finished the second chapter. Each time the reason was the same. About three quarters of the way around the room I called on Anthony, one of the two Dominican boys who were just starting with us that fall. He looked right and then left, seemingly torn as to how to answer. With his dark eyebrows lifted, it looked like he was wondering—should he please these adults so important and powerful in his new life, or try to bond with his new housemates? "I read the whole book," he said in an apologetic voice, "but I did find it awfully boring." Anthony, a sensitive, artistic teen, had solved his dilemma in a way that gave us a first taste of his way of dealing with conflict.

After that aberration, the roll continued with one boy claiming he had only read the first three paragraphs. What's next, I wondered: "I only read the first three lines"? But this last boy was more creative. He hadn't read it at all. "I read the description on the back cover and I decided it was too boring to read."

Interspersed with this recitation were jokes about how to pronounce the author, Jon Krakauer's, name (John Cracker, they'd say) accompanied by many guffaws. At one point in the progression around the circle I, noticing the rosy glow on Wes's face, said, "Hey you guys, this is one of Wes's favorite books."

"No, it isn't that," Wes said. "But I did like it."

Wes, Jay and I held a postmortem and concluded that at least some of the boys had probably read a sizeable part of the book. Over the next few months we overheard snatches of conversation that confirmed that. But the boys never admitted this; it seemed a badge of honor not to.

A couple of years later at an academic committee meeting, Wes again said that the program had enough surplus to buy each boy a book or two for the summer.

The man who was then co-chairing the committee said, "Fine, we'll need some suggestions on what book to get them."

Wes and I looked at each other and, as one, said, "Oh, no! Let the boys choose their own books."

Welcome to ABC

When Edwin and I were talking for this book toward the end of his senior year, I promised him that no board member would know what he told me until after he graduated. Then I braved asking him if there was hazing in the house.

He said there was a tradition of beating up on the freshmen—not badly, just roughing them up a little. Then he contradicted himself by saying that Peter got it bad. One time, some older boys had tossed Peter into the snow wearing only his boxer shorts. Peter told Edwin, "It's going to happen to you."

"Hell, no!" Edwin replied. "It's not happening to me. Do something to me and see what happens! I'm going to fight you."

Edwin sometimes got into fights when hanging out at home in New York, but he preferred to avoid fighting if he could. "I say, 'if we can talk about it, please, let's talk about it.'"

And Edwin didn't get hazed—except for one night. On that night, Peter and Sam came into Anthony and Edwin's room just before midnight. Edwin said that the boys frequently go to each other's rooms after curfew to visit after the staff members are asleep. Peter sat on Edwin's bed and Edwin thought how nice it was to have a visit. They started talking. Then Peter asked, "Do you know what tomorrow is, man?"

"I didn't know. 'Is it Friday?' And I was happy; it's the weekend."

Sam said, "It's Friday the thirteenth."

"So I said, 'Oh, it's bad luck day, that scary stuff.'"

Peter said, "Naw, it's Freshman Friday!"

And then, "They just jumped on me. I was ready to fight. Then they both picked me up and slammed me on the bed.

You know, people always ask why are the beds always broken? We say, 'I don't know. I just lay there and I sleep.'

"Then Anthony woke up and said, 'What the hell!' And he tried to defend me and they said, 'You're not a freshman.' But then they said, 'You're new, too,' so they slammed him on the bed. They were tickling us. But it was nothing bad."

Edwin went on to say that instead of hazing each other in the house, they started playing pranks on prospective students when they stayed over for the night.

"You what?" I nearly choked. I am a member of the board's student selection committee. The previous couple of years we had offered positions to several students who turned us down. We had speculated that it was because the national ABC staff had made the whole process more competitive among public school programs, but maybe this had something to do with it, too.

Edwin told me that one time he, Anthony and Jonathan poured hand lotion on the face and hands of a prospect when he was asleep. It woke him up and then they told him that another student, Joss (not his real name), who was asleep, had done it—then they handed him the rest of the jar of lotion. The prospect went into Joss's room and, thinking that he was feigning sleep, poured the entire bottle on his face. Laughing, Edwin said, "And he wasn't even in the program yet!" That new boy did end up accepting a position in our program.

When another prospect, Tobi, visited, Edwin and Anthony hatched a prank with Elvis. Tobi was sleeping in Elvis's room on a mattress on the floor. Anthony and Edwin each hid in a separate closet in the room. "The plan was to scare the crap out of him in the middle of the night." After Tobi was asleep, Elvis gave a signal from his bed, and Edwin started banging on his closet door. Edwin quoted Tobi as saying, "What the hell is that?" After it got quiet again, Anthony banged on the door to his closet. Edwin jumped out of his closet, at which Tobi let out a loud yell of surprise. Then Anthony jumped out, making Tobi yell out again. Edwin said Tobi laughed afterwards, but at the time he was really scared.

When I thought about these playful episodes, I concluded that any prospective student who decided this was funny was probably well equipped to withstand the challenges of living with a bunch of other teenagers. I didn't ask Edwin what they had done to any of the boys who turned down our offer. I didn't want to know.

To My Boys

Resident director Hayat Omar urged the boys over and over to watch each other's backs when they were out of the house. They could have their differences in the house, but when they were in school or out in the community, they were to think of themselves as brothers. Later resident directors also encouraged this.

Once, a classmate at the school was bullying one of the ABC freshmen, Alan (not his real name), at school. Alan, a slight boy, had a disability that left him no use of one arm. After being hassled for days, Alan struck back and the two boys ended up in an outright fight. Reportedly, Alan, in spite of his physical disadvantage, ended up the best in the fight by head butting the other boy. School authorities suspended both students for a week, and we sent Alan home to his family for that week.

A few days later I was over at the ABC House when Wes Bradley, then head of the executive board, said to a small group of us, "I am concerned that this situation not spread further. Our hothead, Edwin, has already threatened the other kid. Edwin told the bully, 'Don't you ever lay a hand on him again!'"

Staff members told us that the other ABC boys were in an uproar. Wes fretted that Edwin, who was the only senior in the house that year, might lead the rest of the boys to take on the bully. Now Wes said to me, "Remember, Edwin was in that fight with the cheerleaders." (This was an incident that happened after school one day, which we ended up calling The Rumble. We'll hear about it in a later chapter.)

"That was two years ago," I said, "and the only time we know of."

"Yes, but he is used to hanging out on the streets at home."

Edwin, who wrote about his homesickness in the poem, "Lil' Brother," when he was a freshman, would certainly come to his brother's defense on the streets of New York. The following year at the annual poetry night, Edwin had read the poem he called "To My Boys." After a stanza for each boy, mentioning why he was special to Edwin, he concluded:

I dedicate this poem to all of you, not cuz I want a prize or cuz I want a toy,
But because I love you all, & cuz you all my boys.

At this point, when we were dealing with the aftermath of Alan's fight with the bully, Edwin had passed through a somewhat rocky junior year, to become a model house leader and a solid student. A few months earlier at the annual Christmas party he had stood up "to say a few words," and delivered a graceful thank-you to the staff members and then to the assembled board members, including thanking them for working hard to find and hire new staff. He exuded pleasure in being the student whom the younger boys looked up to, and in representing them as a group.

But this day, I knew that Wes was worried about the boys doing something to hurt the program in the eyes of the community. We tell the boys that they are ambassadors for the program. If they cause trouble, we remind them that we rely on donations from the community to support the program. Without that they'd all have to go home.

But I had a counterbalancing worry. If Alan were the target for a bully, would the school be able to stop it? I remembered that in the case of my friend Adele's son, who also has a disability, the administrators at his school were not able to protect him from a persistent bully. Adele felt that the school officials started blaming the victim, telling her that her son just needed to fight back. That message clearly contradicted the school district's policy of zero tolerance on fighting. Eventually, Adele and her husband, at considerable financial sacrifice, moved their child to a private school where he had a second chance and thrived.

In this case, ABC and Lower Merion High School were supposed to be Alan's second chance. In some atavistic corner of my soul I secretly wished that a couple of our older boys would take the bully aside and beat him up.

I was relieved that Alan's problem was resolved peacefully, with skilled intervention from a high school administrator and a school counselor. But I am left wondering if Edwin's threat to the bully didn't help, too. However much his response might make us uncomfortable, wasn't Edwin's behavior a kind of leadership?

If I were a kid, I'd want Edwin watching my back.

Bonding with Staff

At the time of these stories, the ABC House staff consisted of four adults, who all lived in the house. There were two resident directors and two resident tutors. The resident directors were usually a little older than the tutors—in their mid-to-late twenties—and had a range of responsibilities: managing the house and relationships within it, dealing with discipline issues, planning outings for the boys, maintaining contact with the board's executive committee and board committees as well as with parents. Most importantly, they worked to foster a family atmosphere. The tutors were typically recent college graduates in a life-transition period, who stayed with us one or two years. Their primary responsibility was to supervise study hall.

Boys' Impressions of Staff

During Charles's second year with the program, one of the resident directors was Matt (not his real name), an African American man, who had a degree in counseling. Charles and Tyrell, still inseparable, both bonded with him and looked up to him. Matt took them places and they felt comfortable talking to him. Charles said that Matt tended to get nitpicky about chores and would make them redo what they had just done. Since money was involved—they didn't get their weekly allowance until the adult on duty approved what they had done for their chore—they'd usually do it over without argument. In spite of this, they really liked him; Charles kept in contact with him through college.

Of Matt, Tyrell said, "he was a good fit for the house. He understood everything we were going through from a black man's point of view."

My impression is that when Matt started the job he kept too much distance from the boys, but gradually he got more relaxed with them. Tyrell confirmed my impression, saying, "He started off on a power trip, but calmed down a lot. He noticed it wasn't working and changed. I got real close to Matt."

Charles also talked about Brian, who was a resident director for two of the three years Charles was at ABC. Brian, a physical therapist, commuted a long distance to his job. Charles felt that even though Brian was not present as much as some other staff members, when he was there, he "really made the effort. The kids appreciated it." I recall coming by the house late one afternoon to a puzzling sight: seeing Brian and one of the boys in the driveway, crouching in a ready-set pose, then sprinting. After watching them go through this several times, I asked what they were doing. Brian explained that the boy wanted to try out for the school track team and he was helping him to prepare.

Tyrell echoed Charles's opinion of Brian. "He was calm. When Brian got serious, we knew we were doing something wrong. The guys liked Brian."

While Tyrell said he got along with most of the staff, he told me a story about one staffer who had recently graduated from a highly selective college. "He was too smart for his own good." One day this man was talking about colleges with Tyrell, Charles and Michael. He told them that the college he had gone to was one of the hardest schools to get into, but then added, "You guys won't have a problem getting in because you're black."

"When he said that, we didn't like him. We wondered if he knew how that felt." Tyrell added that this was the only real issue he ever had with a staff member. Michael independently mentioned this incident. Three years after it happened, it still stung.

Boys remember special favors that individual staff members did for them. Charles recalls fondly the tutor who gave him considerable help on his college applications, and Peter mentioned that when he arrived as a freshman without having done the assigned high school summer project, several staff members helped him to get it done the first week of school.

One of the duties of the resident directors is to hold weekly house meetings that everyone in the house attends. Those meetings are usually short. Edwin described them as staff asking, "'Are there any problems in the house?' No. The staff will tell us we have to be neater; we have to be more organized, whatever. And that's it." However, if the boys have something they are bothered about, they'll bring it up.

When a boy or a few boys are in trouble, sometimes the other boys will defend them at house meetings. When Edwin, Denzel (not his real name) and Peter got into a street fight and the police came—the incident we called The Rumble—the other boys, led by Elvis, stood up for them. They had handled the situation the same way they would have at home, the others argued, adding that it was no big deal. Several boys told us that what counts most is when a boy who is very respected by the staff speaks up. Several boys mentioned Charles, who with his calm presence was always looked up to, and Elvis, whose leadership qualities became evident in the house, in this context.

When the boys are really mad or upset about an issue, especially if a new regulation has been handed down, a group punishment enforced, or a student is being kicked out, they hold their own house meeting—just the students, no adults. They gather in one of their rooms after the staff has gone to bed and discuss what to do. Edwin said, "Seniors or the older cats usually make decisions about what we are going to do. Then we'll all talk about it."

Since our staff turns over every few years, the boys often have to adjust to one or two, sometimes four new staff members when they return from summer break. For example, during Charles's three years at ABC there were eight different staff members. The turnover didn't particularly bother him. His attitude was "let's see who's next." Charles is a calm, self-confident person, and there was important stability during his years: Hayat was there all three years and Brian was a resident director for two of them. Charles got along well with both of them.

Charles said kids could really tell who is committed, and who is just using the job to figure out what to do next. "If you are living with somebody, you really can't hide that. When the kids spot someone who doesn't seem to want to be there, the boys just don't respond to them."

Michael told us that when the program gets new staff members, he tries to predict what they'll be like. "Most come in thinking this is more of an institution rather than a home environment. If a staff member says, 'you listen to me, you have no say,' they have trouble."

Both Elvis and Michael said that each staff member understands the rules differently, and the guys realize there will be a transition period while they learn the rules and how they are implemented. Michael said, "A lot of what they need to do is not on paper, and they need to figure that out. That is the hardest part. A good staff member is someone who can be flexible. It definitely varies from year to year and from person to person."

Elvis said that one big issue is staff members' pet peeves: each has particular things he or she doesn't like. "I think what we do a lot in this house is compare them to former staff, sometimes behind their back, sometimes to their face."

For all their complaints about rules and having to adjust to different staff members' styles and expectations, the boys develop real affection for some of them. The boys were unanimous in liking Hayat. Edwin said, "She held things together. Nobody wanted to disrespect her. I don't know if it was her background in psychology or what, but she just knew us. We could come into the house and we could've had the worst day, but we would have this mask on so nobody could tell, and she'd see right though it. She'd say, 'If you want to talk?' and you'd still be defensive, 'There's nothing wrong.' And she'd say, 'Now listen, if there's anything wrong, you can talk to me.' Without knowing what was going on or nothing," Edwin snapped his fingers, "she'd just pick up on it."

"Was she a good listener?"

"Yeah, and that, too. Sometimes when you try to talk to some of the staff or even some of the board members you would begin to explain something and they would jump in with the input. And it was like, yo, listen to me, hear me out. It was like they thought they knew the answer right away. But Hayat, she took it all in, all in. And she would evaluate it. Sometimes she'd even say, let me think about it, and she would come back to you after she thought about it."

"When we got in trouble she punished us like she expected us to learn from it—not like a little kid but like a young adult."

"Did she explain why she was disciplining you?"

"Well, sometimes we did stupid stuff, so we knew why."

As an example of some "stupid stuff," Edwin told me about when he and Peter got caught letting a girl into Edwin's first floor room after school. They were all in the same Spanish class; the girl had come over to the ABC House to help them, and she just stepped into the room. Edwin said he knew he was not supposed to have a girl in his room, but thought no staff member was in the house. "Sure enough, Hayat comes in. Peter already had the girl experience the year before, when he had four girls in his room. Peter dashes out of the room with his hat pulled over his face and I'm sitting there saying, 'Hayat, it's not what it looks like.' I had never used that line before. I've always seen it on TV and I'm thinking, man, how you going to use that line, and sure enough I end up using it. She said, 'Just get out; just get out of the house. I need to think.' We were scared because we thought we were going to get kicked out. I was a freshman. It was my first or second month here."

Edwin and Peter stayed away for a couple of hours. When they returned, Hayat sat them down and explained why having a girl in their room was "such a big deal."

"She said, 'Do you understand what's wrong? Look, I'm not going to flip out about it, but you have to understand that in this area if you guys get caught with a girl and she accuses you of rape, you really don't have any protection.'" Edwin said she explained that they don't have the money or resources to go to court and that it would be hard for a black or Latino boy in this area to defend himself.

I was especially interested in how Hayat explained this to the boys. As board members, we focus on the risks to the program—our ability to fundraise and even stay in the community—should a boy get publicly accused of something as serious as rape. And we explain our concern to the boys in those terms. Hayat's focus on the risks to the boys themselves was more sensitive to them, and more appropriate.

For punishment, Hayat made them do everybody's chore for a month, all eight or nine chores every Saturday and Wednesday. All the other boys got their allowance for doing their chores even though Edwin and Peter were doing them.

Michael summed up the boys' feelings about Hayat saying, "She was the queen of staff."

My First Duty Weekend

Jay tells the story of how he started working at ABC in his own words:

As the hour hand quickly made its way toward six o'clock on a Friday afternoon in September, my stomach fluttered with metaphorical butterflies, but this must have been a migration of Monarchs! It was my third week on the staff of ABC, and I was facing my first weekend on duty. I had just graduated from Haverford College a few months earlier. Already, college seemed a distant memory. No more parties, trips, or all-nighters. I was in loco parentis or "in the place of a parent," as a board member had already informed me, but I was wondering if I was more "loco" in the Spanish version of the word! Was I up to dealing with eight lively teenaged boys all by myself for a whole weekend? After the third or fourth boy said, "Jay's on duty this weekend!" I wondered what they had in mind for me.

Six o'clock came, so I gathered with the staff and students for a typical Friday night dinner that consisted of breakfast foods: pancakes, sausage, and eggs. While others at the table wolfed down every bite on their plates, I picked at my food, more concerned with which student was assigned to clean up the table. Unsure of what to say, much less do, I listened quietly to the dinner conversation, already a lively exchange about the event of the evening: the first school dance of the year. I noticed the eagerness and uncertainty on the faces of Elvis and Michael, who were freshmen, while recognizing the confident poise displayed by Charles and Tyrell. Would any of them view me as an authority figure of any kind? Would they be home by their curfews? Only 10:00, 10:30, 11:00, and 11:30 would tell.

Minutes later, the guys occupied all four of the house computers, instant-messaging friends, family, and girlfriends. I wondered—what happened to picking up a phone? Is this a typical Friday night? I had imagined intense card games, Monopoly, and the boys hanging out in the living room. I resigned myself to watching a television channel left on by the students: a Japanese animé cartoon.

My stomach was in knots that a Boy Scout could not untie.

The doorbell rang.

I bolted up from the sofa, wondering who could be at the door on a Friday night.

As I rushed through the entrance hallway and pulled back the door, I saw four cute, giggling girls standing on the porch. They must be here for the older boys, I thought.

"Hello. May I help you?"

"Is Elvis home?"

Elvis! I guess our quiet Elvis takes after his namesake. I could not help but smile as I called out, "Has anyone seen Elvis? He has visitors."

Immediately, Elvis appeared and, just as quickly, was gone, the first of the ABC students headed to the dance. The others soon followed.

Again, I found myself eyeing the clock. In the unusual silence of the house, I began to think that a lot of people my age were probably out dancing and having fun. Was I having fun? I thought I knew what fun was, but did I? I was nervous, weighed down with responsibility, and desperate to connect with these teenagers.

Another ring sent me lunging from the sofa again. This time it was the phone. One of the older students proceeded to tell me his story, justifying why he should get a curfew extension. Since I had no one to consult, I gave him a half hour extension. I gave it with a tone that I hoped conveyed an underlying threat with dire consequences if the curfew was broken. The "what-ifs?" and "what-should-I-do's?" dizzied my head, then Elvis and Michael came through the front door. Two down and six to go! Within the next two hours, all of the guys returned, using a five-minute-give-or-take approach to their curfews. Too exhausted to debate such details, I closed that heavy storm door. I felt like I had pulled an all-nighter and it was only eleven o'clock.

"Good morning, Jay!" Elvis said, as I walked through the kitchen at around seven o'clock the next morning.

"Elvis! You're up!" I said with a degree of shock.

"Why are you up so early?"

"Laundry," he said as he headed to the basement to check on a load of clothes.

With my appetite restored overnight, I sat down with a bowl of cereal. Soon, I heard slow, heavy footsteps trudging up the stairs.

"Jay, you won't believe this! The washers are broken!"

"What? No way!" Clink! My spoon hit the bowl and disappeared into the milk. So much for breakfast. I bounded down the stairs to see Elvis's clothes afloat in gallons of water in both washers. I had no idea what to do. Elvis peered over my shoulder at the mess. At the time, I wished that I could have suddenly transformed into Tim Taylor from "Tool Time," but I couldn't and Elvis could sense it. I was just my green self. I picked up the phone to call staff members, all of whom were away from the house. Hayat answered the phone and suggested that I check the phone book for someone to come and take a look at the problem. No one could come until the next week. In the meantime, Elvis would have to drape his clothes all over the basement to dry. And he would have to figure out what to wear the next day when he would meet his host family for the first time.

As more of the guys woke up, I opened doors and windows to let light into the house. About that time, a pulsating sound got my heart racing. This time it was neither the phone nor the front door-bell. The fire alarm was going off! But where was the fire? I barreled into the kitchen to see if anything was burning. Nope! Completely empty. I could only envision fire trucks zooming down the street and fire fighters interrogating me as to what in the world was going on. Not sure of what to do, I went into the office. I searched through a drawer of unmarked keys for the alarm key. None of them seemed to fit.

Soon, Michael, a freshman, came into the room. "Jay, what's going on? Don't you know what you are doing?"

At this point, I could not hide it. "No. In fact, I need your help. None of these keys seems to work!" Just then, a middle-aged lady rang the doorbell to ask what was the matter.

"Do you need help?" she asked with a concerned look on her face.

How should I respond? I thought. Should I project "the man of the house image" or should I proceed with a wailing, tear-soaked confession? I need help in so many ways. But instead, I said, "We're just searching for a key to turn off the alarm. But thank you!"

After she left, I called an ABC board member. In a feeble attempt at maintaining a calm tone amidst the blaring background, I said, "This is Jay from ABC. As I am sure you can hear, the house fire alarm is going off. I have searched for the key to open the case to turn it off. I can't find it. Do you have any suggestions?"

"Well, Jay, didn't you learn what to do at staff orientation? You should know how to do this." I felt my confidence level plummet into the red. This is just great! I have no idea what I am doing. I have annoyed a board member. As I looked back at Michael, he moved yet another key into position. And click! The fire alarm case opened, bringing the sweetest silence that I have ever heard. I could have held Michael above my head like winning teammates do in a sports movie! Instead, I plopped down on the sofa, too exhausted to move from it for the rest of weekend. I could not hide the real me from the guys, the board, or anyone else anymore. I was a newborn staff member who had just experienced a baptism by fire alarm.

The next evening during study hall, Michael came to me for help on an English project. As he handed me his poem, I looked up at him and thought, Hey, he must think that I can do something right!

House Trip to the Jersey Shore

The year that Jonathan was a freshman, Monica, then resident director, announced at a house meeting that everyone would be going to the Jersey Shore for a weekend in late May. "She said, 'Pack your bags because as soon as you get out of school, we're going to head down.'"

Jonathan had never been on amusement park rides before—not while he in lived Puerto Rico as a young child, and not in New York City. The only time he had stayed in a hotel had been when executive board member Rob Howard had taken all the boys on a college trip through New England the previous fall. From time to time the staff takes the boys on excursions such as camping weekends or to play paintball, but this was their first one that year. "I just wanted school to end that day," Jonathan said.

Edwin told Jonathan several times, "Dude, we're going to have so much funnel cake when we go to the shore." Eating funnel cake, a Pennsylvania Dutch specialty, was something else Jonathan had never experienced.

On the Friday of the trip, he remembered, "We were all pretty tired from the drive, but that night we went to the boardwalk and just walked around. It was cold, and there weren't many people there. We were all just goofing around. Michael and Elvis were off on their own being seniors, but the younger boys stuck together and the staff followed along behind us."

That was the first time they saw the video game Dance Dance Revolution (DDR), the music video game that gets you dancing by following arrows shown on the screen and reflected on the floor: up, down, to the left, to the right. Jonathan said they spent about an hour doing it. "Edwin's a good dancer and is super at it." At curfew, Jonathan was so tired he went right to sleep.

After breakfast the next morning, they went back to the boardwalk. "It was sunny and the amusement park was open for rides. It was so much fun to have the staff acting like kids, going on rides with us." All of the boys and some of the staff went on bumper cars. "Everyone was taking out aggression on each other, but it was a lot of fun."

At lunch Jonathan, who has quite a sweet tooth, ate funnel cake—a lot of funnel cake. Right afterwards he went on a roller coaster. "I was so sick. When I got off I told everybody to walk ahead of me and I put my head down near a garbage can and just sat there till the nausea went away. Too much fried dough!"

Jonathan also went on a Ferris wheel with Edwin. "I was really, really scared because you were up in the air, high above the ground and it swings side to side." I asked him if he had ever been on one since. "No!"

Although Monica had planned the trip, another staff member, Dean (not his real name), was micromanaging it, telling the boys where they could go, what times they had to meet. He had given money to each boy to go on rides and to play arcade games. Jonathan said, "I ran out midway through the day. I thought, dang! I spent all my money. We were like, 'Dean, can we have some more money?' He gave me twenty extra bucks, but that was it. He said, 'Be cautious about where you spend it now.'"

That afternoon they all went back to the hotel and swam. "Saturday night Dean paid for us to go on go-carts. They are pretty much faster bumper cars."

On Sunday on their way out of town, the staff took them to another, less crowded beach for a couple of hours. They played football, threw Frisbees and walked the beach. Jonathan said, "The water was so cold I didn't want to swim, but Edwin, who is Mr. Adventurous, would just jump in the water."

I asked Jonathan what was good about this trip. "Getting out of the house. We really needed some time away from the house. We had all felt a lot of tension. There had been episodes between a couple of students and arguments that happened constantly throughout the year. We were super grateful to have such a good time together." Jonathan said that the tensions mostly disappeared after they got back to the house.

The boys had enjoyed Dance Dance Revolution so much that Monica purchased the video game for the house. In the weeks after the trip, every time I stopped by in the afternoon, I would see two or three boys dancing in front of the living room TV. The happy vibes lived on.

La Resistance

Jay was feeling relaxed as he came home from work one spring evening. For weeks the boys and the staff had been at loggerheads over the use of the house computers. Staff tutors kept catching a few students using email and instant messaging during study hall, when they were supposed to be working on school assignments. And some students were monopolizing computers. After weeks of nagging and bickering with the students, the staff drew up new rules. Students would now have to sign up for time, limited to one and a half hours, to use computers during study hall. Only two students at a time could be in the computer room during study hall hours.

The staff had announced the new rules the night before at the weekly house meeting attended by all staff and students. Charges of "That's not fair," and "That's group punishment," flew around the room. In the heated discussion, students and staff kept repeating their opposing points. The students left the meeting incensed, but the rules stood. Jay felt confident that he and the other staff—Hayat, Tim and Monica—had solved the problem.

That evening Jay trooped into the house foyer, stopping by the mailboxes to get his mail. That's odd, he thought; his name was upside down. Checking, he saw that all the names were upside down. Walking further down the hallway, he saw that the letters on the announcement board at the end of the hall were rearranged. He turned into the living room. All of the artwork was hanging upside down. What the hell is going on, he wondered. He crossed the living room into the computer room to see if some of the boys were hanging out there. Surely they could explain this. No boys were there, but the lampshades on all the desk lamps had been screwed on upside-down. Jay turned back into the living room and walked through the dining room—where pictures also hung on their heads—on his way to the apartment he shared with Tim. A dry-erase board sat precariously atop the doorframe to the apartment. Neatly inscribed in marker was the following message:

> Unjust laws exist: shall we ABC Students be content to obey them, or shall we endeavor to amend them, and obey them until we have succeeded, or shall we transgress them at once? Men generally, under such a government as this ABC Staff, think that they ought to wait until they have persuaded the majority to alter them. They think that, if they should resist, the remedy would be worse than the evil. But it is the fault of the government itself that the remedy is worse than the evil. It makes it worse. Why is it not more apt to anticipate and provide for reform? Why does it cry and resist before it is hurt? Why does it not encourage its citizens to be on the alert to point out its faults, and do better than it would have them?

Henry David Thoreau would have been proud, Jay mused. He wondered, who was responsible for this? It must be one of the two juniors who were studying American literature. Which one? Was this a solo endeavor or were all the boys involved? More to the point: how should the staff respond? The ball was clearly back in their court.

About a year after this protest, Jay and I talked to Elvis and Michael, who were now seniors, about what the boys had dubbed La Resistance. Since Jay was no longer on the staff, they were willing, indeed eager, to talk about it.

In the house meeting the boys had argued hard for their case, but as Michael said, "There are certain times when no matter what you say at a house meeting to staff, they are not going to change it. We knew that." After school the next day some of the boys, while grumbling about the new rules, decided to stage a rebellion. The major issue they resented was group punishment for individual infractions. They wanted to do any small rebellious things they could think of. As a boy would toss out an idea, he would then go do it: turning the pictures upside down, the mailbox labels, and on and on.

Elvis said, "Michael had this really dumb idea. He put tape over a keyhole [to the locked office]. He said this will stop them for a while."

Peter had coined the term La Resistance for the rebellion. This was the title of a song from the TV show South Park. Elvis said, "Peter kept playing it over and over in the computer room and he'd be dancing and waving his arms around."

Elvis admitted he made up the sign; he had been reading Thoreau in class at the time. Elvis and Michael told us that most of the boys were involved, except the two seniors, but they, Elvis and Michael, were the ringleaders.

Michael said, "The staff probably saw it as a joke, but one or two of the staff were really mad about it."

The staff left the pictures and many of the other things upside down. Eventually the boys righted the lampshades after a board member told them that it was bad to have such strong light shining in their eyes. However, the new computer rules stayed in place for the rest of the school year.

In their conversation with us, Elvis and Michael reflected on what they viewed as rebellions in the house and said that the boys stage about one a year. Elvis said, "We only consider it a rebellion when you have the leaders of the house, that is those guys most liked by the staff, support what you are doing.

My freshman year there was one instance where Charles was really arguing with the staff at a house meeting about something." At the time Charles was the only senior. Elvis went on to say that nothing went beyond that house meeting, but the other guys looked on it as a rebellious meeting, and they felt supported by Charles.

Michael said, "Some people like to try to take it to the extra level. They like to do something that will get them in trouble. The point of it is to do something that won't get you in trouble."

We soon understood that Elvis and Michael had carefully calibrated what they could do that would express objection but not get any of them punished. At the time of La Resistance, some of the other boys in the house, in particular one senior, were frequently pushing limits and tweaking the staff. One of them drew down punishment on a regular basis. Elvis and Michael had steered a careful course through their time at ABC, keeping their objections enough under the radar to escape punishment. That they mentioned Charles's behavior three years earlier suggests what a strong role model he had been. The mature and even-tempered Charles, too, never got himself in trouble during his years in the program.

At the time of La Resistance, Jay and the other three staff members didn't know about what once had been a yearly ritual. In the dreary, cold days of January or February, the board would receive a letter from the students that listed grievances they had with the staff and concluded with something to the effect of, "We respectfully request that you fire all of the staff."

Common Language

Jay reflected on his experience as a staff member in this way:

I came to Haverford College from Bybeetown, Kentucky, a small town that stands in stark contrast to the affluent Main Line area on the outskirts of Philadelphia. On first sight of Haverford, I thought I was in a big city. I did not understand the idea of a suburb since most urban areas in Kentucky, such as Lexington, more accurately resemble the surrounding suburbs of Philadelphia. When I told this to the guys, they laughed in disbelief. Their first impressions of Ardmore were very different. Most were bored by the slower pace and lack of things to do. Their perceptions shocked me.

No matter how different our experiences, sharing them always helped us understand each other. In addition to stories, we touched upon our backgrounds through poetry. I wrote a "Where I'm From" poem to read to the guys.

> I am from one out of 120 counties and I am one less
> Resident in a small town of less than 120.
> I am from a Madison County with bridges Hollywood
> Would never even consider for a movie.
> I am from the world-renowned Bybee Pottery,
> Clay and potters wheels, spinning, spinning,
> Through fingers, molding, shaping that from which
> Water is poured or food is eaten or candles burned.

The allusion to the "Bridges of Madison County" movie drew a few chuckles. The bridges in my poem were nothing like those you find in New York. In fact, I was awestruck the first time that I drove over the Brooklyn Bridge, a bridge familiar to all of the guys. It was so high up that I thought I'd throw up. I was terrified by the volume of cars zooming past me. Nevertheless, I had bittersweet memories of the bridges in my town. I had fished, lost a neighbor in a fatal car crash, and cleaned up as part of a community service project for school on them.

I can't tell you how many times I heard, "Jay, where's your accent?" from the students when I told them I was from Kentucky. Usually, they followed their question with a funny rendition of a Southern accent. I answered that I had lost mine as an undergraduate. So, it is no surprise that, as a staff member, I immediately picked up on the street slang used by the guys. It was so different from that which my family spoke at home.

I am from southern-drawl-drawn-out-vowels,
A no-need-to-hurry-take-your-time-way-of-speaking,
Pop instead of soda, buggies instead of shopping carts,
Sweepers instead of vacuum cleaners, sacks instead
Of bags, "Yes Mams" and "No Mams" and churches,
Preachers, sermons, holy rolling, and Sundays
When all the stores in town are shut down.

Another part of my heritage that I shared with the boys was The Kentucky Derby. Each first Saturday in April, I would make the guys watch The Kentucky Derby. "All of this hype for a two-minute race?" The guys could never quite get over this aspect of the event. I had never thought about it like that. In keeping with the competitive spirit that permeated so many of the activities around the house, I would pick a horse and prod the others to do the same.

I am from horse farms, bluegrass and black fences
Stretching, derbies, triple crown winners,
Secretariat in 1973, Seattle Slew in 1977,
Affirmed in 1978 (the year I was born)
And no winners since. I am from placing bets,
Believing in the underdog, beating the odds,
Risking losing it all, losing it all, stories of almosts,
Sunday Silence, Strike The Gold, Go For Gin,
Silver Charm, Funny Cide, and Smarty Jones.

Although I never picked a winner, one boy chose Funny Cide in 2003. He had beaten a Kentuckian at his own game.

Since many students in the house had relatives in the South, I found that we shared a common love for certain types of food. We made sure that fried chicken was frequently on the house menu. In fact, any type of fried food worked for us. Dinner, often called supper in the South, had always been an important part of my family. It was also an integral part of life at the house. Everyone had to be present at six o'clock each weekday night.

> I am from Grace before meals, collard greens,
> Fried chicken, biscuits and gravy, grits, country ham,
> Green beans, corn on the cob, red eye gravy, corn bread
> Hominy, iced tea and lemons, chicken and dumplings,
> And seconds, and thirds, and "Don't be bashful, boy!"

As with Southern culture, I found that many of the cultures in the house such as Dominican and Puerto Rican also encourage multiple helpings of food. Needless to say, we helped ourselves to food each night.

When I heard the students talk about life in the projects and the 'hood, it changed my entire image of poverty. Prior to college, I had lived at the foothills of the Appalachian Mountains, and I had only known the poverty I had seen there. Urban life seemed like that and then some. My admiration and respect for the boys grew.

> I am from mountain shadows and lives cut off
> From the rest of the world, poverty, an absence of plumbing,
> Outhouses, third, second, and first grade educations,
> And, quite often, no educations, rotting one-room
> School houses, trailer parks with too many stray dogs
> And cats and raining cats and dogs and flooding
> Rivers and streams, tornado warnings and watches,
> Sirens, army depots, incinerators, chemical weapons,
> The distant thumping of World War II bombs being
> Destroyed, constant fear of nerve gas leaks, evacuation plans.

I shared a picture of my grandmother's outhouse with the guys. Again, hysterical laughter followed by questions. "Did you really take a smash in there? How did you flush? Didn't it stink?" I never thought that an outhouse could be so interesting.

Home was a place that made me feel isolated in college, yet my appreciation for home deepened at ABC. Seeing the guys' pride in their homes encouraged me to do the same. Why hadn't I had more pride in where I was from in the first place?

I am from honeysuckle and morning glory vines
Twining around fences, hummingbirds and the scarlet
Glow of their feeders in the evening light, empty beer cans
In ditches, tobacco in the fields, or hanging in barns, or burning
In the cigarettes of my mother or my brothers, smoke, smoke,
And heavy fogs, and ghosts, hauntings, stories, oh, those stories
That are still haunting me. I am from there is no such thing as
    a stranger,
Waves and hellos, hugs, pats on the back, offers to rest, relax,
Take off your shoes. I am from a homegrown wisdom far greater
Than anything I have ever learned in a classroom or ever will
    for that matter.

The truth is that my love for home was there all along. It's just that I had never embraced it until I embraced the cultures of the ABC students. In order to appreciate others, you have to appreciate yourself. It was a powerful lesson. In fact, of all of the things we learned from each other, one piece of wisdom still remains strong, as the last line of my poem emphasizes:

No, I will never forget where I am from.

Bonding with the Larger ABC Family

It truly "takes a village" to run our A Better Chance program. When they arrive, each student is assigned an academic advisor, who helps oversee his academic progress through his four years with the program. Sometimes these are board members (I served as Anthony's for his time with us, and for two years for Jonathan), but more often they are just members of the community. We also match each student with a host family, with whom he spends at least one Sunday afternoon a month. In addition, students come in contact with many of the program's board members, particularly chairs of the academic and house relations committees, and members of the three-person executive board.

A Home away from Home

Once a month each ABC scholar spends Sunday afternoon with his host family, and returns to the ABC House after an early dinner with them in time for seven o'clock study hall. If all goes well, the relationship continues for the four years of the boy's time in the program. In many cases, the bond is close enough that significant contact continues for years after the student graduates.

The makeup of the families who volunteer to be host parents varies widely. Some, such as the couple who were Tyrell's host parents, have young children and the family enfolds the boy into their activities. In other cases, hosts are couples whose children are grown. Such was the case with Edwin and his hosts, Patricia and Nino Silva. Cuban immigrants, Patricia was an elementary school teacher and Nino, retired.

Edwin told me, "The first time we met we spoke Spanish, and I thought, wow, a little taste of home. I felt so comfortable. It felt like I was visiting family in Connecticut. And when I was leaving she said, 'Mi hijo, date vuelta,' my son, turn around. And she made a cross on my forehead, like my grandmother used to. So I asked her, 'Bendición, Mama,' I ask for your blessing, mother. And she gave it to me. 'Que Dios te bendiga.' Every time since then, always, always, always."

When he was a freshman, Edwin called his host family more than once and asked to come over in addition to his monthly visit. "You remember," Edwin said, "I was homesick—like a dog! I didn't feel homesick when I was with them.

"Sometimes I would just hang out with them. We'd talk Spanish. Have a cup of coffee. I don't drink coffee, but I would have it just to socialize. She would be cooking some rice and beans. And chicken. And it smelled just like home. They had paintings by Spanish artists and books in Spanish and wow! What we'd usually do: she would cook, we would eat, it would be lunch. Then they'd say, 'Let's go to a movie.' They were movie people. They'd have a suggestion, but if I wanted to watch a movie, we'd go watch what I wanted to watch. And then they'd take me to the ABC House."

The Silvas stayed on as Edwin's host parents for his four years with ABC. On a sunny Sunday afternoon, the year Edwin was a senior, I was standing in the ABC House kitchen with Wes Bradley at the end of the graduation party. Patricia Silva joined us and said, "I always give him a blessing when he is leaving." Responding to our puzzled looks, she explained, "It is something Spanish mothers do with their children. I thought, he's all grown up now, so I wasn't going to do it. And he said"—her eyes misting up here—"'Mama, aren't you going to bless me?'"

Michael's host parents, Rex and Meg Goldberg (not their real names), were to play an even more important role in his life, but for Michael the relationship didn't get off to an auspicious start. The first host-family Sunday, they were out of the country. "I thought, Oh man, I have a great host family and they're in Greenland!" Rex had been a staff tutor with ABC when he first graduated from college, and they had hosted several ABC students afterwards.

When they got back from Greenland, Rex and Meg picked up Michael one day to get acquainted. Michael remembers, "They were playing Run-D.M.C. on the car radio. It's an old rapper from the eighties. And I was thinking, I hope they aren't playing this for me. I don't like this music. Then Rex started singing with it and I decided he must like this stuff."

Things rapidly improved. "Most host families tell you what you're going to do. Whatever I wanted to do, I got to do. It was my time. We'd always do something cool. We went to movies. We went to see a battleship. We went to a rodeo and we all hated it and left. We did lots of stuff."

Sometimes they all just hung out at the Goldberg's townhouse in Philadelphia's Center City. Michael liked when Meg cooked. She had worked as a pastry chef for a few years at Le Bec Fin, Philadelphia's most elegant French restaurant, and is a superb cook. Now Meg was helping Rex build the business he had founded. Michael said, "Sometimes if I had a lot of homework, we did homework. They'd help me if they could. College application time, we spent multiple host-family days doing college applications."

The Goldbergs, who at the time had no children, took a stance familiar to any good parent of teenagers. "They've always told me that if I am in trouble at any point, call them no matter what time it is. I know without hesitation, that if I need anything, they're there for me."

As an example, Michael told me that one time a girl from New York City was visiting him and he took her to meet Rex and Meg. "She got stuck in Philadelphia because Greyhound wasn't running anymore that night. And I didn't have enough money for Amtrak. She needed to be home by the end of that night or her mother was going to be a very unhappy person. Rex and Meg gave me fifty dollars or whatever it was to pay for the train."

RIGHT: *Jonathan in the ABC House yard (photograph by Sharon Sherman)*

BELOW LEFT: *Elvis dressed for his prom*

BELOW RIGHT: *Edwin in the ABC House*

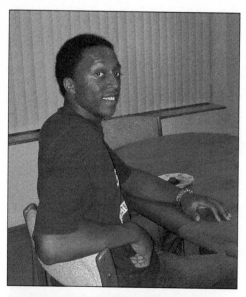

LEFT: *Tyrell visiting from college and eating Patty's brownies*

BELOW: *Anthony in the backyard of the ABC House (photograph by Sharon Sherman)*

Peter as a senior

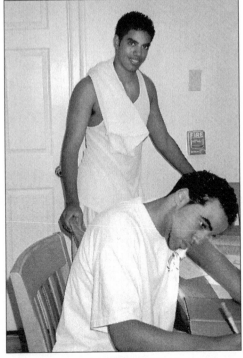

Anthony (LEFT) *and Edwin
at study hall*

POETRY NIGHT (CLOCKWISE FROM TOP LEFT)

Jonathan reading his poem

Jay (LEFT), *Hayat reading a poem*

Jay (LEFT), *Edwin* (CENTER) *and Hayat*

Anthony reading his poem

CHAPTER 5

Study Hall

One evening midway though our monthly board meeting, we enjoyed a surprise visit from a well-dressed African American man who was an alumnus of our program. He had graduated from college, earned a master's degree in business, then started his own business and was doing quite well. We had been immersed, as usual, with the problems and challenges of running the current program, and his visit offered a welcome respite. Rob Howard, who was chairing the meeting, finally asked him, "What was most helpful about the program?"

After a long, reflective pause, he said, "I hate to say this. I never would have at the time. But I'd have to say study hall."

Study hall. Ah, study hall. It is at the heart of the success of our program. It is also the bane of the boys' lives. Five evenings a week, from Sunday through Thursday, we require the boys to do homework and study under adult supervision from seven until nine-thirty. No TV, no video games, no telephone calls, no surfing the Internet, no emailing, and supposedly, no, or very little chattering among themselves.

A few relatively mature and strongly motivated boys accept this discipline easily. But every few years a fourteen-year-old freshman arrives who has a serious case of "ants in his pants," or "motor mouth" or worse—both in the same body. Most of the boys in the program fall somewhere in between these extremes.

Compounding the problem, most of our boys made good grades in their middle schools with very little time spent on homework. Our study hall routine presents a major challenge.

Two live-in staff tutors, usually young adults who have recently graduated from college, supervise study hall. They work at day jobs or attend graduate or professional school. Their dual responsibility is first to keep the boys focused and working and second, to tutor in topics where they are well trained. We also have the good fortune of access to undergraduates at nearby Haverford College who will come over, usually once a week, both to help out generally and, if needed, to tutor in a subject such as a science or higher-level math that can't be handled by current staff.

Study hall takes place in the downstairs public rooms: the dining room, the living room, the small music room off the living room, and especially in the computer room/library which is a long, narrow, converted sun porch, ringed on three sides by windows. Sophomores and upperclassmen who are on the school honor roll earn the privilege of studying in their rooms. They need only to come downstairs to use a computer or reference books in the library. Some boys love this prerogative and spend most of study hall time in their rooms. (Currently, Lower Merion High School provides each student with a laptop, so the situation is somewhat different.)

Staff tutors are usually grateful for having a couple of boys who study in their rooms because it eases their task of keeping order. For some boys—such as Jonathan, who is sensitive to noise and people distractions—this privilege was golden. However, Charles told me he rarely studied in his room although he always had that choice. "It was more fun to be around the guys." Raised in a household of women, he loved being in a house full of boys.

"Study hall is definitely necessary for doing well at Lower Merion," he told me, "but it was never that intense, so it was fun." He thought some of the rules were pretty strict. The staff wanted them to work and be quiet for the entire two and a half hours. Charles said there was no way the boys were going to do that. They never actually planned on breaking the rules as a group, but all of the boys took breaks—going online, instant messaging—or lingering in the kitchen after a snack break. "We realized it was hard for them to punish everyone."

Jay remembers that Charles would amble down the stairs from his room on the second floor, then lounge on a living room couch. Then he might walk around, talk to another student, usually Michael, and try to get something going, maybe rile them up. Jay said that Charles was such a quiet presence that the staff tutors usually ignored it or laughed it off, unless the boys got really loud.

When Edwin was a sophomore he told us that even if he had attended an undemanding high school at home in New York, he probably wouldn't have earned as good grades as he did at Lower Merion. The reason: he wouldn't have had study hall, where he had to do his homework; instead he'd probably be spending his time hanging out on the street.

We talked about it again a few months before his high school graduation. Edwin said the structured time of study hall is good. "But, I'm not going to lie. Sometimes we have three hours of homework but sometimes we have an hour's worth. It's like; I want to be a regular kid. Let me go out and play, let me talk on the phone, but they say, 'No, you have to pick up a book and you have to do this and that for another hour and a half and shut up!'" This last was delivered with a laugh.

I asked Edwin if there were any games he played on the staff to get around this. He said staff would always say that if the students are using the computers, they need to be doing schoolwork. He liked to use a certain computer that sat at the short end of the computer room. While the screens of the other computers were easily visible from the doorway, the screen on this one was not.

Edwin said once they'd finished their homework, he and other boys often played computer games, emailed, sent instant messages, checked blogs, or generally played around on the computer. "They rarely catch us because we develop skills." The boys get used to different staff members' routines. For example, of the staff tutors at the time we spoke, the boys saw one man as pretty laid back. He rarely checked what they were doing if they seemed busy at a computer. However, Samantha could be relied on to check. "You know what to listen for. As soon as you hear her feet coming down the stairs, you go back to your work."

When Edwin was still on the computer after he had finished his homework, if he heard Samantha coming, he'd pull up an old document on the screen. "It could be a paper I wrote last year. I just start typing random words. She thinks oh, he's working, he's working. As soon as she turns around, back to the game, back to instant messaging."

I have unbounded empathy for our staff tutors who have to keep a whole roomful of teenaged boys quiet and focused on schoolwork night after night. Several years ago when we were short-staffed for several months, I helped run study hall a couple of nights a week. Three freshmen were not adjusted to the routine. In addition, one of our juniors, a very sociable young man, frequently and easily distracted two of the sophomores. One night I sat at the long dining room table alongside several of the boys, congratulating myself on having finally browbeat them into being quiet. Then, one boy farted. Giggles burbled along the table. "Sorry," said the offender. "I couldn't help it." I feigned not hearing. A few minutes later another boy farted. Snorts joined the giggles.

"Guys!" I said in my best schoolmarm voice.

"It was an accident." More sniggers as his housemates supported him. Of course, it continued for the rest of that night's study hall. Of course, I resorted to watching the clock, longing for nine-thirty to arrive and set me free.

I asked Jay how he dealt with the challenge of keeping guys from talking too much or walking around during study hall. His answer surprised me. He said he didn't find it helpful to confront them and to ask, "Why are you talking?" Instead, he found it more effective to take one student aside and ask, "Okay, what do you have to do?" He would ask the student to get his assignments out and would start talking to him about them. He found that it broke up the talking and the boy responded to the individual attention.

Jay went on to say that the boys feel bossed around when a staff member tells them to stop talking or messaging friends. Jay thinks that they respond better to a nurturing approach. He tried to be like a big brother, and show he was willing to share his human side. While a disciplinarian might be able to establish a presence right away, Jay felt that for his approach to work, you had to be there all the time for the boys, and be consistent in how you worked with them. It was a slower process, but built respect.

When I first met Jay, I sensed he was an unusually gentle person. His method of tutoring must have grown out of the kind of person he is, and perhaps explains why he bonded so well with the boys

CHAPTER 6

Expressions

During the time that Hayat and Jay were ABC staff members, writing poetry became a major way that the boys expressed what they were experiencing as teenagers and as ABC students. But they found several other ways to do this as well. Journal writing, drawing and painting, listening to music, and even taking part in sports all became expressive and emotional outlets, ways for them to enrich their lives and to balance the demands of academics.

Friday Night Poetry

In addition to being a talented athlete, Elvis had a sensitive and reflective side; he arrived at ABC already liking to write poetry. Serendipity landed him with two staff members who could nurture and celebrate that interest. Hayat Omar, newly promoted to be a resident director, found poetry her chosen mode to make sense of the world. Jay Fritz, recently graduated from Haverford College, had composed a collection of poems for his senior thesis.

When Jay started his job with us, nervousness and insecurity radiated out of him, but his eagerness to help the boys and be a friendly presence was palpable. He started posting poems on the walls of the kitchen and the dining room for the boys to read and as a way to engage them in conversation. Sometimes he tacked up his own poems, but mainly he put up published poems he thought they would enjoy reading. Supervising study hall formed the core of Jay's job for his first two years. When helping the boys with homework writing assignments, he was in his element. I remember being over at the house during study hall several evenings and hearing boys use Jay as a dictionary, calling out, "Hey, Jay. What does . . . mean?"

Hayat, a nurturing young woman, often gave the boys pep talks about striving to better themselves and feeling good about their accomplishments. She wrote inspirational essays for them and talked about writing poetry as a way to express feelings.

Partway through that first year, Hayat and Jay started hosting informal poetry readings on Friday or Saturday evenings when they were on weekend duty. They would sit and read poems, their own or those of established poets, with whomever of the boys were hanging around the house. They invited the boys to read aloud favorite published poems or their own writing. Sometimes they discussed the meaning of a poem, but mostly they just took turns reading.

Because Jay stayed around the house so much his first year on staff, he was usually there for the readings even when he wasn't on duty. Indeed, the boys took to saying, "Jay, get a life."

The older students were usually out attending social events with friends from school, but the younger boys regularly took part in the readings. That year the three freshman, including Elvis and Michael, regularly attended these readings. One or two sophomores often took part as well. Hayat purchased a copy of Tupac's *The Rose that Grew from Concrete* for the house library, and the boys devoured it.

By the spring, poetry writing had become such a cherished activity that Hayat decided to hold a surprise poetry night for the ABC board members. In April—which is National Poetry Month—Rob Howard, who was then head of the executive board, asked all the board members to assemble in the living room following the monthly board meeting.

There, one by one, the boys stood and read a poem of their own composition.

Hayat prevailed on a few board members to be judges. I was a judge that night, and we had to throw out many of the categories she had given us and make up new ones. While she had chosen several humorous award categories, most of the boys' poems spoke of serious issues such as homesickness, trying to fit in, or wondering about the meaning of life. After the judges allotted a poem to each category, Hayat passed out awards and hugs to each student. We left that evening in a happy glow, and found it such an emotionally satisfying evening that it became an annual event. Jay continued to organize it each year after he left the staff.

Homesickness is a popular topic for new students. During his freshman year, Elvis read us this poem he'd written:

Why is Each Day a Struggle?
Why is each day a struggle?
Why aren't people helping me to find the answer to where
I'm going in life?
Why is it each time I want to see my family I have to
Look at pictures or count the days till I'm home again?

And every time Momma calls I have nothing to say,
But when she hangs up, I talk to her picture,
Wishing I was little again and had Momma's arms to run into.

I still remember running to Momma's bed when I had
Nightmares, and how Momma would hug me and put me
To sleep next to her. Momma felt so warm, and there
Was never a bad dream when I was in Momma's arms.

Momma's a hundred miles away now, and Pops says I
Gotta be strong for the family. He and Momma love me
Too much for me not to succeed in life, and I love them
Too much to let them down.

In addition to his homesickness, Elvis stressed himself adjusting to the high expectations at Lower Merion High School. Partway through his first year his father, who owned and ran a hot dog stand in Brooklyn, fell and broke both of his legs. He was unable to work. Around the same time Elvis's mother, who works in food services, became seriously ill and was also unable to work. The family had little income coming in. Elvis thought he should return to New York and work to bring money into the household. His parents insisted that he stay at ABC and concentrate on his education.

Elvis was known in the house as a workhorse, whether for staying up late to finish all of his homework, or lifting up couches to vacuum underneath when he was doing his house chores. I remember talking to a staff member at the time who told me he thought part of the reason that Elvis worked so very hard was that he felt guilty about his good opportunities when times were so tough for his family. When Elvis went home for the summer, he worked at the hot dog stand. Eventually his mother returned to work.

While Elvis arrived liking to write poetry, his fellow freshman, Michael, had never written poetry before coming to ABC. When his English teacher gave an assignment to write a set of poems inspired by Harper Lee's *To Kill a Mockingbird*, he was quite nervous about it and turned to Jay for help. He struggled with the form, but soon he was writing poems for pleasure. He produced a sizeable collection—about half of them love poems.

Jay remembers one evening when he was helping Michael with a poem, but had to leave for a staff meeting. When he returned an hour or so later, Michael showed him these lines:

The Final Touch
It was very easy to feel the stillness of the
night. It felt like lightning hitting me with all
of its power. I know Dora was feeling it, too.

As fast as it came is as fast as it went,
because the sun came out and put light
on me. I could feel its loving warmth and happiness.

Michael was writing about a girl at home that he was in love with. But the line, "As fast as it came is as fast as it went," could well be a motto for our time with the ABC boys. They are with us for four years, but often it seems the years whiz by in a blink. This is the short time we have to help them reach their dreams of getting to college and preparing to flourish there. The boys who were with us during the three years of the poetry era left with a bonus: an appreciation of reading poetry, a heightened sensitivity to language and, for a few, such as Michael, a form to express themselves for the rest of their lives.

The Solace of Writing

When Hayat became resident director, she gave each boy a blank notebook and encouraged him to write in it regularly about his feelings and worries. Most of the boys wrote in these journals just now and then. However, Charles, who was then a senior, remembers writing in his fairly often at the start of study hall. For Michael, who appeared so friendly and cheerful to everyone, the journal became an emotional lifeline. Into it he poured out the loneliness he felt, writing about adjusting to a new school and a new environment, spilling his heartache onto the pages. "There were times when I would write in my journal and cry. I'd put crying in parentheses."

A few months before coming to ABC he had begun dating Dora (not her real name) and had fallen in love for the first time. Hard. His journal from his first months at ABC was full of longing for her. When he started to write poetry, it became another avenue for expressing his feelings. Many of his early poems are about Dora or are addressed to her.

There is Only One Star in my Heart

There are galaxies full of
Stars. But only one caught my
Eye. This star was the brightest.
It made me feel something that
No other star has ever made me
Feel. It was the feeling of love.

One of the ways Michael used to keep in contact with Dora was to write in a notebook and mail it to her. Then she would write something and mail it back. At the time, our program did not allow the boys to have cell phones, a policy later reversed largely thanks to Michael's tactful lobbying.

After several months, Michael decided that a long distance relationship wouldn't work, and he broke up with her. His portfolio of poems includes one full of ambivalence and regret about this. The first lines read:

When I broke your heart
You never wanted to speak to me.
You said never to call, but I called anyway. . . .

Eventually, Michael and Dora agreed to remain friends. Michael continued to write in his journal throughout his time at ABC, although not as frequently. He mostly reserved it for times when he was troubled. Although he had not written poetry before he came to us, he continued to write poems and, consistent with his well-organized, careful personality, he printed out all of his poems and kept them. He thought he would continue to write poems for the rest of his life.

I asked him what effect he thought the emphasis on poetry writing had had on the house. "This may be far fetched, but I think poetry calmed everyone. Students are often mad at something or mad at staff. Living in a house with twelve or thirteen people is hard on anyone. For me it was very soothing to write."

Michael said the emphasis on poetry was most concentrated during his freshman year, but continued to some extent as long as Hayat and Jay were on the staff. When we talked about this, there was an entirely different staff. He said, "Right now no one really does it any more. No one is enthusiastic about it, but at that time it was just spontaneous."

Several years later, when Jonathan was a senior, he was in the school choir and was quite excited about auditioning for an after-school a cappella choir. When I asked him a couple of days after the audition how he did, he said, "I didn't make it." After a pause, he continued, "I had to write in my journal a lot that night. A lot!"

This startled me because I had not heard about journal writing in the house since Hayat had left. I told him that I hadn't realized the current staff was encouraging journal writing.

"They're not. Michael gave this to me when I was a freshman and told me to use it to write my thoughts about being here in it." I asked him if Michael had given one to each of the younger boys and he said, "No. Just to me. He told me I was the most deep thinker of the boys, so that is why he gave it to me."

I don't know if Michael continued to use his journal as a way to cope with stress after he graduated, but he had clearly given guidance to another ABC student.

I need to tell Hayat how her gift continued on.

Anthony: Our Artist

When Jay, who was no longer on the staff, arrived at the house one April evening for the monthly ABC board meeting and annual poetry night, Anthony grabbed him, saying, "I need your help. I haven't finished my poem yet." Jay followed him down the steep stairs to the basement where Anthony was working on a project for art class. Told to do a life portrait and to use his imagination, Anthony had chosen to paint a life-sized self-portrait in medieval armor. A helmet did not cover the head, and he had drawn his own tumble of satiny black curls as if the wind rushed through it. A dramatic slash of black recreated his eyebrows. Down the sword he wrote the words *Yo Sobrevire*: "I will survive." Anthony continued to work on the portrait, while dictating his poem to Jay. Later that evening, Anthony stood before the assembled board members, staff and other students and read the following.

Father Where Art Thou?

Sometimes, I wonder, are you in eternal slumber?
Why ponder if I haven't seen you since I was younger?
I asked for you, then my sister, too.
My Mother said you were through.
Damn! I wish you were here to see how much your boy grew!
If it's not too much to ask,
I'll forgive your past.
I know that years have passed.
Your face in my mind is blurry,
But, at least, your memory I carry.
Guess what? Right now, I'm a little hairy.
My sister plans to marry when she gets thirty.
My mother moved to another country.
Where have you been all of these years?
If I see you, I wouldn't know if I
Should cry in tears or run out of fear
At least one thing will remain true:
Father, I miss you.

Bendición Papi

Until that evening, Jay had never heard Anthony speak of his father. Nor had I, although I was his academic advisor. A week after that poetry reading, while I was talking to him about his time at ABC, Anthony suddenly opened up.

He told me about a day when he was six years old; he still remembers what he was wearing: a pair of raggedy gray jeans, once black, and a yellow shirt. His mother, whom he barely knew, appeared and told him they were going on a trip. "The next thing I know, she had me in court for two hours. She was getting custody."

Anthony's mother had moved to New York City when he was two years old, but he stayed in his native Dominican Republic living with his father and his paternal grandparents. His grandmother acted like a mother to him until he was five and moved to New York. Anthony remembers his grandfather warmly as the man who was always giving him pizzas and M & M's. His grandfather owned a successful auto repair business, and Anthony told me that the family owned land and farmland.

Anthony's mother worked in New York as a home health care worker. Eventually, she took his younger sister to New York to live with her, and later sent money to his father to come to New York with Anthony. The two came, but Anthony's father decided not to live with her; instead he moved in with another man and took Anthony with him. "He sort of kidnapped me," Anthony said.

His father worked as a mechanic, but he and Ray, the man he lived with, liked to party and drink and would spend most of their money on that. Somehow, Anthony's mother managed to find where they were living. After she appeared on that fateful day, Anthony only saw his father once in a while when he showed up to visit. Anthony treasures memories of trips to an ice-skating rink and gifts of ice cream. When Anthony was nine his father stopped coming. He had not seen him since. Anthony still had contact with his paternal relatives in the Dominican Republic; but they didn't know where his father was either.

With typical generosity of spirit, Anthony said, "I owe my father some thanks because in the future I'll be a better father figure."

Anthony, his mother and sister moved every year: around New York City, then to Allentown and eventually to Baltimore. Every year Anthony attended a different school. The year they lived in Allentown, when he was in middle school, home was with seven other relatives in a two-room apartment. Actually, it was a one-room apartment that some family members subdivided to give it a small living room. "My family is very clever. Sometimes when there were not enough beds, they'd lay a pile of clothes on the floor, put a blanket over it and we'd have a mattress!"

If home was not a place, Anthony's heart was very much wherever his family was living. He worried about not being in Baltimore to supervise his younger sister and keep her out of trouble. He worried about not being there to bring cups of tea to his mother when she was ill, as she often was. During the years that Anthony lived at the ABC House, a slightly older male cousin lived with his family; but in Anthony's mind he, Anthony, was the male head of the household, the reliable caretaker.

Anthony's talent and passion for art emerged when he was a small boy living in the Dominican Republic, and he decided he wanted to fly in an airplane. How fun it would be to see "the trees from atop." He thought that if he drew an airplane, it would turn into a real one. He drew a squiggle. Nothing happened. More squiggles, still nothing. But he was not a boy to give up easily. He tried again. And again and again. His drawings got better, looking more like an airplane, but none of them turned into something that flew.

However, one day when he was five years old, he did get to fly in a plane when his father brought him to the United States. By this time Anthony loved to draw. He had watched his father, grandfather, and some of his uncles draw and paint. Now he could, too. One uncle earned extra money drawing cartoons.

Anthony found life in America difficult. He didn't speak English and was put in bilingual classes. He longed to speak English fluently and "giggle like normal six-year-olds." His mother expected him to do many household chores: cooking dinner, cleaning the kitchen, mopping the bathroom. "Sometimes I would look out the window and wonder why the kids playing outside were not doing their chores."

His imagination helped him to escape from his troubles, his art becoming a balm. He had not lost his fascination with flying, and he loved to paint strokes of blue on white paper, his attempt to capture the sky.

Given the opportunity to take classes in Lower Merion High School's strong art program, he pursued his lessons with intensity. During the spring of his first year with us, a board member arranged for him to get a scholarship at the local community art center, where he took additional drawing classes after school.

Anthony's dreaminess had become familiar to us—even when he was in a group he often appeared to have his mind somewhere else. He was notorious for turning in homework assignments late. I was his academic advisor, and when I chided him about this he was always polite, but my scolding never changed his behavior. However, when he was talking about art and especially when he was working on a piece, he was totally engaged and focused.

The first time I took Anthony to an art museum, the famous Barnes Foundation, I felt as if I had a personal tutor of a most unusual sort. He pointed out techniques that were specific to a particular artist, "See the sharp edges Cézanne uses." And "Renoir uses that brush stroke a lot."

"How did you learn that?" I'd ask him.

"I just study the paintings," he'd reply. Since Anthony came to us already knowing these things, I assume he was mostly self-taught. While I am used to art lectures that emphasize style or themes, it was a new experience to walk around with someone totally focused on the how of the art—someone who was an artist himself.

Music

One fall, melodies from Alicia Keys' "Song in A Minor" filtered through the rooms of the ABC House almost every weekday afternoon when the boys returned home from school. All the guys in the house, including staff members, had crushes on her. They swooned over her vocals, especially the parts that Jay described as "extraordinary soulful high notes with the soft pressing of piano keys."

The boys held frequent discussions about how beautiful she is, when her next album would be out, and which song was her best. When MTV did a segment called "The Diary of Alicia Keys," all the boys sat glued to the TV set.

In a project for his art class, Anthony had painted a self-portrait in armor, with a woman standing behind him dressed to look like the Virgin Mary. When I asked him if that was supposed to be Mary, he answered, "No. It's Alicia Keys."

He was shocked when I asked who she was, rushed me into the computer room, opened a website he had book-marked, and showed me several pictures of her, saying, "Isn't she beautiful?"

Michael wrote a love poem about her.

Listening to music was a major and valued pastime for most of the ABC students. At times boys ran into conflicts with the staff over how loud the music was played, and some-times over the verbal content of rap songs they played. But mostly they were allowed to listen to what they wanted, and they often walked around with earphones attached to a por-table CD player.

Edwin did this frequently, but even when he was not obviously listening to music it often looked like he was hearing it in his head, for he would do a few dance steps as he ambled along, dancing through life.

While some of the boys were quite specific on what kind of music they liked, Edwin's taste was catholic. In a poem he wrote for Poetry Night when he was a junior, Edwin, who enjoyed so much street life at home, explained this.

My Music

Coming from them gritty streets of New York City
You'd expect me to listen to hip-hop from Diddy and
Biggie
Yet living in the Lower Merion Area,
You'd expect me to bang my head with rock hysteria

With parents from the Dominican Republic
You'd expect me to blast merengue, bachata, and salsa
In public
But having roots from Africa, the mother land
Continent,
You'd expect me to listen to music with drumbeats, and
Be real content

Well let me tell you all right now,
All of it is my music yet none of it is my music.

I mean, you'll see me every day pop lockin to hip hop
Or two steppin to Spanish music
Just cuz I got a big spirit and I need to defuse it

But when you want to judge me
Don't judge me by what I listen to
Because, honestly, all music is the same
Just 1 and 2

And with this said, I want you all to know that
My music is the beat that comes from my heart,
Because without it my world would just grow apart.

So listen to all those sounds of music
Because those beautiful sounds are your music,
Those beautiful sounds are my music.

Gentle Charles, a tall basketball star, had listened mostly to Gospel when he first came to ABC, but he said he liked some rap as well. Still, when I asked him by email, when he was a college senior majoring in philosophy, the name of the song that he, Tyrell and Michael had listened to in their own private ceremony for his graduation, I was surprised by his response:

The name of that song is "Juicy" by Notorious B.I.G. . . . It's my favorite rap song of all time. Like most rap songs it does have a few curses and uses a few words that many consider negative; however, if one is able to get past that, beneath lays a very accurate social commentary and also a very empowering message. So I'm just going to explain a little why we like the song and how we view it.

First, the artist who recorded the song is from our hometown Brooklyn. As I am sure you have seen during your time with the boys through the years the ones from New York tend to be very proud of where they are from. So already we relate to the artist because he comes from the same place that we do . . . [It] can be seen as a metaphor . . . that he came from the same or at least very similar social and economic backgrounds as us. In many ways he was us and in many ways he was worse off than we were.

Even in the inner cities Notorious B.I.G. was looked at as a failure. The low-of-the-low so-to-speak. He was a high school drop out, a teen father, a drug dealer (all of this is expressed in the song) . . . He was in many ways the anti-American dream. He was poor, uneducated and black and in the midst of all that he was also unattractive and overweight; he was cross-eyed. Everything about the Notorious B.I.G. would seem to say failure from the outside. Despite these circumstances, B.I.G. "made it." He became a success even by American societal standards. He gathered up enough drive to not just make it but to become arguably the great M.C. of all time . . .

Each of us saw a little of B.I.G. in ourselves. The state of growing up in the inner city is in many ways a state of defeatism. And B.I.G. was saying through his song, forget what society tells you, I made it, me, the anti-America. B.I.G. and "Juicy" embody what it is to come from Brooklyn and to make it in whatever you do. He was talking about rapping but it is applicable to whatever path one chooses . . ."

Basketball: A Dream Deferred

Sports can also help students express their emotions in meaningful ways. When Marjorie called to invite outgoing Tyrell down for an interview with our program she asked, "Have you ever heard of Kobe Bryant?" Silly question to a thirteen-year-old, urban African American teen, but she knew this was a major selling point for our program. She explained that Lower Merion High School was where Kobe had played high school basketball. Furthermore, the co-captain of the basketball team with him was Jermaine Griffin, who was an ABC student.

When Tyrell first arrived for his interview, he was skinny and stood about five-foot-four. None of us had any idea how brightly basketball burned in his soul. By the end of his first year with us he had grown several inches, and by his senior year he had comfortably passed the six-foot mark, and was broad shouldered though still skinny.

While most of our boys play a sport—football, track, even cheerleading—basketball wins first place in their affection, hands down. The boys spend a lot of time after school and on weekends shooting hoops at the back end of the house driveway and at "the Shack," the community center just across the street from the house.

I, however, have mixed feelings about this passion. When we have boys on the team, I fret all through the season and especially during midterms. Basketball season runs right through midterms in January. On a game night, the basketball players don't get home until ten or eleven at night, missing study hall that night, and often need to take one or two exams the next day. More often than not, the boys' grades suffer at least a little that semester.

Tyrell, however, held a different view of it. "During basketball season I missed study hall a lot. I'm an advocate of playing sports at school because that helps your time management. School lets out at two-thirty. Say we don't have practice till five-thirty. You come home. You got to make sure you get your work done because you're not going to be in study hall. So I'd make sure I did something when I was home."

One game near the end of Tyrell's senior year climaxed his high school basketball career, and he wrote this essay for his English class about it.

My Dream Deferred

I bleed orange and sweat Gatorade. My calloused hands resemble the grip from my basketball and the air in my lungs is the same air that fills the ball. It's been this way since I was 8 years old, the year I was introduced to the love of my life, the game of basketball. Growing up it was obvious what my dream was, to play in the National Basketball Association, for I tried to do everything to live that dream. While my childhood friends were out getting in trouble, I was practicing my jump shot on my homemade basketball goal. Everywhere I went I carried my basketball, I even slept with it at night. Nothing was going to stop me from getting to the NBA.

Playing in the NBA was not always my number one goal. That came three years later. My first goal was to beat my brother Zack in a game of one on one. Zack was actually the one who introduced me to basketball, and he's the reason why my number is 20 (his number is 10 and my goal is to be twice as good as him one day). For three years we played one on one everyday, and the same thing happened each time. Zack would easily beat me, and it seemed with each loss, I got more determined to keep trying. All that losing was worth it, because the day finally came when I could "do the impossible." I don't know what got into me; I guess I just got tired of losing all the time. I remember playing that game as if my life depended on it. I won 21-20, and I thought, "If I could beat Zack, I could beat anybody." I just knew I could make it to the NBA.

Fast forward to my senior year in high school: the end of my last basketball season and still no college recruits. "If it's meant to be, I'll get scouted," is what I keep telling myself, yet it's February and no recruiting letters or phone calls. By this point, I wasn't even worried about the NBA, just taking the Lower Merion Aces as far as we can go.

Fortunately, we had a chance to play in the PIAA District I semifinals at Temple University's Liacouras Center versus Coatesville. This was the biggest game that I ever participated in. There were over a thousand fans in attendance. I admit I was nervous and so were my teammates. So nervous that we fell into a seven point deficit going into the fourth quarter, and throughout the quarter we didn't gain an inch on them until there were two minutes left. During a timeout, I began to realize that this game was the closest I was ever going to get to living my dream. This was it; this was my NBA. Right after that thought left my mind I took a deep breath and looked down at my hand. What I saw scared me at first. My palm looked like an actual basketball. I closed my eyes to adjust my vision, reopened them and it was gone. However, I looked at the back of my hand and my sweat had a yellowish tint to it; I thought it was just the lights in the arena. At that moment, I wiped my mouth with my hands and some of the sweat went into my mouth, and to my surprise it tasted like Gatorade. Everything began to make sense. It was time to make the best of living my dream.

Following the timeout, I scored 6 unanswered points before I tripped, fell, and cut my knee. I had to exit the game to get cleaned up, but the whole time I looked at my knee in amazement because I saw orange blood trickling down my leg. When

I returned to action, we were down one point and I was fouled with under 45 seconds left. I made both foul shots, putting us up by one point, and I knew we were going to win that game. But, just like I knew I was going to the NBA, it didn't happen. Coatesville heaved up a prayer that went in to win the game. I finished with a game high of 17 points.

After the game, I sat dejectedly in the locker room holding onto my sweat soaked jersey. The taste of Gatorade was no longer in my mouth, my hand looked normal once again, and my bandaged knee held red blood. I'm not saying I lost the love for the game that night, but I gained a better appreciation for it. I just got finished living my dream; it was just deferred a little. So I wasn't in the NBA, nor will I ever make it there. I'm satisfied with what I've been able to accomplish. Living a deferred version of your dream is better than not living your dream at all.

Cheerleading

My husband and I were eating in a restaurant in Philadelphia's Chinatown with Tyrell, who had graduated a few years before, when I asked him, "Have you heard? Cheerleading is the current passion at the House."

Tyrell's face registered shock. "You're putting me on!"

"No, no. She's right," my husband said.

A bit later Tyrell told us, "When I was playing basketball, if another team had boy cheerleaders we'd try to get our fans to make fun of them."

When I interviewed Charles, who had also been a basketball star in high school, he said he had heard the news. Later he said, shaking his head, "I can't believe it! We went from the house having basketball stars, to cheerleaders," his voice a sneer.

I should not have been surprised at their disapproval, because it had been clear all year that several of the men on the board were quite uncomfortable with this new passion among the guys. Where in most years they talked enthusiastically about the students playing basketball, football or running track, and often attended the games, now some radiated a palpable sense of unease.

Peter, ever the adventurer, initiated the cheerleading. Jay remembers his saying, "I am going to start something new here," when he tried out for the squad during the spring semester of his sophomore year. Not only had no ABC students ever been cheerleaders, in no one's memory had there been boys on the Lower Merion squad. Peter talked Edwin into joining him for tryouts.

Edwin played baseball on the freshman team that spring. He loved baseball, which he had played in a park in his Dominican neighborhood in New York. However, the attitude of many of his teammates frustrated him. He felt that they didn't take the game seriously and didn't work hard at it. Many of them, he thought, just wanted an activity to list on their college applications. He knew that the same boys, with most likely the same attitude, would be on the team when they moved up to varsity. Since he had already become good friends with Peter, he agreed to try out for cheerleading. When fall rolled around, Denzel (not his real name), a freshman ABC student, joined them on the squad.

The boys took up weightlifting so they would be strong enough to lift girls in stunts. Peter had grown by that point to about five-five or six, but was still slightly built. Edwin was five-nine and, while muscular, was slim and fine boned. Denzel looked more like a linebacker than a cheerleader, but was impressively agile and graceful.

Soon the walls of the house echoed with the sound of their practicing cheers, and they liked to show off routines, especially jumps. Denzel bragged to me several times that cheerleading had a higher accident rate than high school football did. That impressed me, but not in the way I think he intended. When I went to one of their exhibitions, I watched boys lift a petite girl high aloft, then toss her air-borne. I held my breath until the girl was safely caught by four teammates.

In late winter the ABC house relations committee made Peter drop out of cheerleading when he got into serious trouble in the house. By that time Jonathan, who was then a freshman, had caught the fever and wanted to try out. I overheard the other boys teasing him that he'd have to be on JV while they were on the varsity squad. Jonathan went about preparing the same way he did his schoolwork, working very hard and worrying a lot. It turned out there was no JV squad, and he was accepted to varsity for the following fall.

Peter rejoined the team at the start of his senior year. The boys on the team all came back to Ardmore early for preseason practice. They had talked a couple of guy friends from school, both African American, into joining the squad as well. There would be six boys and twenty girls on the team.

They all went to a preseason cheerleading camp in the Poconos for a few days. One night Peter got caught in the girls' side of the camp after curfew, and the coaches kicked him off the team. Board members shook our heads at Peter once again showing up in the wrong place with girls, and once again going a little too far. Months later, Peter told me that he wasn't the only guy who had been over in the girls' area that night—just the only one who got caught. Loyal to his male teammates, he didn't tell on them. He rejoined the wrestling team that year.

Later Edwin described the camp incident in more detail. "We were all at a party on the girls' side. I started running because I saw some girls from our team coming. I'm saying, 'Peter, let's go, let's go.' But he's an idiot! Peter's dancing on top of a table with ten girls around him. He's twirling his shirt over his head and he keeps dancing. So I ran away.

"One of the girls on our team didn't like Peter, so she went to get the coaches. When Peter saw them he ran into the woods." The coaches went to the boys' room and asked where Peter was. Edwin said, "We told them, 'Ah, he's taking a shower.' So they went in the shower. He's not there. We say, 'Ah, we don't know where he is.' When Peter came back we say, 'Hey, Dude, your ass is in trouble.'"

That February, the Lower Merion cheerleading squad qualified to go to the national competition in Orlando, Florida. There they placed eighth out of fourteen in their category, one position away from qualifying for finals. They spent the rest of their trip visiting Disney World. Only a few teams had boys on their cheerleading squads. Thousands of girls attended the competition.

Edwin told me, "There is this stereotype that male cheerleaders are gay. So when the girls saw that we're not gay that just blew them away. So we got a lot of attention. A lot!

"Not only that, there's not a lot of inner-city kids who are doing cheerleading. When they saw these dark-skinned kids wearing do-rags and the braids and they talk different. Woo! And they can dance and all that! We'd go to the pool. Fifty girls around us. We'd go to eat. A hundred girls around us. We're celebrities, man! I'm thinking, this is why I'm doing cheerleading. But it got to the point we got too much attention."

Edwin said that the Lower Merion coaches didn't trust them because of the incident with Peter at cheerleading camp, so they took the hotel room next to the boys and put a parent chaperone in the room on the other side. The night before the competition, all of the kids slept quietly, but the next night, girls kept knocking on their door.

"They were really loud, laughing, giggling. And they'd say, 'Let us in, let us in.' Then Jonathan would open the door just a little and say"—Edwin dropped his voice to a whisper—"'Go, go, go! You're going to get us in so much trouble. The coaches are right next door.'"

They got very little sleep, but the boys didn't want to leave Florida. "The girls wanted to come back to their boyfriends, but the boys could stay for two more years." Here Edwin stretched out his arms wide.

"It was guy heaven!"

CHAPTER 7

Crises and
Turning Points

The ABC students face many challenges in their years with us, including some dark times. Family issues back home, chafing under house rules, self-doubt, the need to keep up with academic work in spite of other stresses—all can take a toll. Do they learn from these? Some students go right to the edge, and even over it. Can they manage to make it through the program and continue on to college?

Learning the Rules

Curfew. Getting to dinner at six o'clock sharp. Doing chores. Speaking respectfully to staff, signing out when away from the house, being on time for study hall, and on and on. When new boys first arrive at the ABC House, they spend a day or two alone with the staff for orientation, to get to know each other—and to learn a sizeable list of rules and expectations. Staff and board members remind them that they are also to be ambassadors for the program in the community.

Anthony remembers well the first few weeks he was at ABC. "I tested the boundaries, but unintentionally. This is how it all goes down. First I went to visit the Radnor ABC House [another ABC program]. I get in trouble, right? Because I didn't call for an extension [of time]. So, then I'm grounded for the whole weekend. Then that Monday Peter, Edwin and I go out and we came in about five minutes late for dinner. Everybody's already eating. I got grounded for another weekend."

A few days later, Anthony and Edwin went out in the afternoon and didn't mark the sign-out board or tell anyone where they were going. Staff members went out looking for them. Once again they got back late for dinner.

Anthony described what happened next: "When we got back home, Hayat gave us a speech. Then for the first time I can remember, the only time, I saw Elvis really mad. He said he tried really hard to get us in here. He actually chose us. And our behavior reflects on him. Then Edwin and I felt very sorry. We started straightening up our act."

Anthony was not used to getting into trouble at home. He told me that after his initial burst of missing curfews and deadlines, "If there is a lot of trouble, you never hear my name."

A few months after Anthony came to ABC, Edwin, who was a freshman, and Peter, already a risk-taker as a sophomore, hatched a plot to sneak girls into the house after school. Girls are never allowed on the second floor, and only allowed on the first floor when a staff member is present. At the time, there might sometimes be no staffer in the house right after school (now, there is adult coverage scheduled for every afternoon). Anthony didn't want to get in trouble, but he also didn't want to snitch on his friends, so he hung out at school for a couple of hours. Peter and Edwin did sneak the girls in, a staff member did catch them, and trouble did descend on their heads.

Even though Anthony managed to steer clear of trouble, one thing he found especially hard was that six o'clock dinner means at six o'clock sharp. In addition to his dreamy temperament, he came from a family that had an entirely different sense of time. The very hardest part of being in the ABC program was that now his whole life had been subsumed into a schedule. "It was never like that at home. At home I could hang out with friends. I could do anything I wanted to do as long as my homework was done, the house was clean and I told my mother. Being here sometimes seems like a prison."

Anthony thought that most of the ABC students find the restrictions really hard; they are used to much more freedom in their lives. I think that is true for many of the boys, but not all. Elvis said that his life at home was much stricter: "I had to ask my mother's permission to open the refrigerator." Many of our boys come from homes where their parents or single mothers fear danger on the streets in their neighborhoods and hold their sons with a tight rein. For these boys, the opportunity to walk freely around Ardmore and surrounding communities represents liberation.

Almost any teenager will, from time to time, need to test limits; a few make a career of this. Then there are boys such as Edwin, who had enjoyed a great deal of freedom in his Dominican neighborhood in New York. "I barely spent time at home. I was hanging out on the street. I could sleep out with friends as long as I told my mother."

Talking about living in Ardmore his first year, Edwin said, "Man, that was horrible. In a city you can get around anyplace you want to on the subway. Here you gotta call a friend with a car. At least now I have friends with cars." Edwin handled his frustration over restrictions at ABC much differently than Anthony did. Edwin, an emotional and impulsive young man, frequently broke rules about being home on time, and sometimes cut classes. He relied on charm, which he has in abundance, to wiggle out of punishments. On the occasions when that didn't work, he accepted his lumps—usually grounding—with remarkable good nature.

In May of Edwin's sophomore year, prom fever coursed through the house. The two seniors, Elvis and Michael, were both going to their senior prom. And Peter, then a junior, was taking a girl who was a senior. Another senior girl had asked Edwin to be her date. While the other boys had rented tuxedos, Edwin bought one for himself with money earned from odd jobs—babysitting and gardening for board members.

Edwin had broken a string of rules that spring, and had cut some classes as well. A week or two before the prom, the board members on the house relations committee decided to punish him by forbidding him to go to the prom. I was appalled. I felt sorry for Edwin, but especially so for the girl whose date was snatched away at the last minute. While I accepted that he needed some punishment, couldn't they have found a less drastic method?

The evening of the prom I joined a few board members and staff gathered in the backyard of the ABC House to take pictures of the boys in their tuxedos. The other ABC boys stood in the driveway: joking, laughing, taking part in the good spirits. In the middle of them stood Edwin, wiry and muscular, in a tee shirt and jeans.

I found myself standing next to him, and I said softly, "I'm sorry about your not getting to go."

He started. "It's okay. I'm cool."

"I know, but I'm still sorry."

"I did wrong. I'm cool," he repeated.

Putting such a brave face on it, I thought—such a good sport, standing out here cheering on his housemates instead of sulking in his room. I reached over and rubbed his back and said, "I know you're cool, but can't I still say I'm sorry about it?"

He momentarily went stiff, then engulfed me in a tight hug, kissing me on the cheek. "Thank you."

We stood together and watched Michael and Elvis and Peter depart for their exciting evening.

Gone Missing

In the middle of a mid-summer afternoon during summer vacation, Wes Bradley called me about a board issue and then said, "Edwin's missing."

"Missing! How?"

"He didn't show up to work last night. His boss called his mother. She doesn't know where he is. Neither does his brother. They're in an uproar."

Edwin. Sweet, sweet Edwin. Every summer when the boys go home, I worry about something happening to them—teenaged boys on mean streets. Edwin, the most street-smart of our boys at that time, hung out with other teenagers in his neighborhood whenever he was at home. This summer he was traveling by subway most nights, to a job cleaning fish at the Fulton Fish Market. Could something have happened to him on the way?

Wes went on to say, "He had a girl visiting him from Lower Merion, and he was escorting her to the bus home on his way to work. He's making good money. Maybe he did something stupid and is with her."

Stupid, but a much preferable alternative than to what else might have happened. We'd hang on to that idea.

"If you hear anything, please call me. Right away." He promised he would.

I tried to put it out of my mind, but, of course, couldn't. Images from the nightly news stole into my head.

A day or so later, Wes called about another board matter and told me, "Oh, there's a rumor that Edwin might be here in Lower Merion."

"Doing what?"

"With that girl. Molly. She'd been visiting him in New York. She's one of the cheerleaders." This said with a tone of disapproval.

I remembered meeting Molly (not her real name) a year or so earlier when I was eating dinner at the house on a night when Edwin had invited her to dinner. Small, blonde and very pretty, she sat at the table quietly but very much taking everything in. What she had to take in was a table full of teenaged guys who were doing the verbal equivalent of riding bicycles standing on their hands to impress her.

She had moved to Ardmore only a few weeks before. Someone mentioned that she had been a cheerleader in another state, and planned to join the Lower Merion team in the fall. Later I asked Edwin if he had asked her to dinner to try to interest her in joining the cheerleading team.

"She's in one of my classes," he told me. "I just asked her because she's cute!"

Molly did join the team the following year, which was both her and Edwin's junior year. Fine boned and petite, she was a cheerleading flyer with amazing extensions and the flexibility of a rubber band. Cute? She was exquisite.

Now, Wes continued, saying, "I hate that cheerleading. I think Molly's a bad influence on Edwin."

"How's that?"

"She distracts him."

Wes was Edwin's academic advisor, and he worried that Edwin was easily distracted from academics by his social life, and by girls in particular. For girls, Edwin was a honey pot.

The news that Edwin might be with Molly allowed me to get some sleep. A day or so later, Wes called again. "Edwin's back home. He had escorted Molly to the bus and just decided to go to Ardmore with her." Wes laughed and continued, "He's not used to having money in his pocket." He went on to say, sounding like a good, concerned father, that Edwin's boss liked him, and he hoped that Edwin had not lost his job.

Wes continued. "I talked to his mother. I didn't actually get to talk to Edwin. He was out, making amends: to his aunts, to the neighbors, to the parish priest."

Peter: All Through the Night

Sleep my child and peace attend thee,
All through the night;
Guardian angels God will send thee,
All through the night.

—Old Welsh lullaby, with words by
Sir Harold Boulton

One December evening at the annual Christmas party, all the gifts had been passed out to the boys when Peter suddenly jumped up and announced there was another gift. He stood in front of the assembled board members, staff and other students clasping two large, flat rectangles to his chest.

Hayat had finished her five years with the program the previous spring. But this evening she was back with her husband, Frank, and her baby, Hana, born the previous spring just before the end of school. Peter said, "I had the honor of taking the first pictures of Hayat and Frank as a family." He then turned the rectangles around to show two identical, framed ten-by-twelve photos of Frank and a smiling Hayat cradling her tiny daughter. He gave one photo to Hayat and the other to Frank.

Well, that's a very generous gesture, I thought, especially for a boy who doesn't have much money. There must be a story behind it.

Peter had arrived at ABC as a chubby five-foot-two, fourteen-year-old freshman. All the other boys in the house were bigger, stronger, and older than he. And taller. Several were six feet or more. Worse, the other freshman was over six feet tall and skinny. Peter felt hazed by a few of the older boys. They told him it was just roughhousing, but he felt he couldn't defend himself. Once when one of the guys sat on his chest, Elvis, then a sophomore, pulled the other boy off. As if the hazing wasn't bad enough, Peter found school much harder than his middle school in Hartford, Connecticut, had been. He was used to getting good grades, and suddenly was struggling to get mediocre ones. "My freshman year was a horrible experience," he said.

English had always been one of his best subjects, but he was having regular run-ins with his English teacher. When the teacher told him he wrote poorly, Peter worked very hard on his next written homework assignment. Then the teacher told him he must have plagiarized it, because she was sure he couldn't write that well. This trauma was piled on top of problems with his family over Christmas break. "I didn't think I was worth anything anymore. I wasn't sure I was even wanted here." That spring he wrote a poem about how he was feeling.

In My Mind

My mind is a path of lost dreams.
Hopes have come and gone.
False beliefs have crossed my path.
I feel this path will lead me nowhere,
where love and peace is to be found.
Torrents of immense strength have tried to knock me down,
but as long as my soul, body, and mind are one, I will not fall.
Lights have appeared,
To try to guide me to safer sanctuaries,
My mind is young and foolish so I am persuaded,
I have tried to settle in places that have disguised themselves
trustworthy and good,
but they are also a torrent of evil power.
I am on a path of never ending possibilities.
Where will I end up no one not even I will know.

So my mind and body are still on the search,
the search for a place that I can call HOME.

One day Peter was feeling especially down. This was a
period when writing poetry was an established method of
dealing with feelings in the house, and Peter wrote a poem
hinting at suicide. Later that evening he showed it to Jay.
Shaken by the content, Jay showed it to Hayat. By this time
it was late evening, and they decided he should go to the hospital for a twenty-four hour suicide watch. When Peter got
wind of this, he ran and hid. He went into a little annex off the
main basement room, squeezing himself into a corner behind
a broken door. Soon the whole house was in an uproar, with
staff members and students running up and down stairs trying to find him, looking in closets, bathrooms, behind beds.
Listening to all the uproar, Peter heard people say, "Let's go to
the park, let's look down the street and see if he's there." He
gave up and came out. Hayat and Jay decided they would take
turns staying up with him and then reach out for board and
professional help the next morning.

Jay took the first shift and sat talking with Peter for several hours. When Hayat took over, she read him poems—
some that she had written during difficult passages of her life.
By then it was well past midnight. After a couple of hours,
Peter said he wanted to go to sleep. She told him that was all
right, but that he must sleep with his door open. She would
keep watch.

Peter shared his room with another student, but his bed
was closest to the door. He remembers, "Sometimes I would
wake in the middle of the night just to check. I would look
outside and Hayat would be reading a book and watching me
from the staircase." When morning came, he looked out and
there was Hayat sitting on the top step of the stairs, still reading, still there. Later, of seeing her there in the morning, Peter
said, "Wow, I didn't think she would care that much."

The next morning the staff pulled in board reinforcements who provided a variety of supports.

Hayat gave Peter a copy of one of the poems they had read that long night. He tacked it to the wall by his bed, and, every night for the rest of the school year, he read it.

Invictus

Out of the night that covers me
    Black as a pit from pole to pole,
I thank whatever gods may be
    For my unconquerable soul.

In the fell clutch of circumstance
    I have not winced nor cried aloud.
Under the bludgeonings of chance
    My head is bloody, but unbowed.

Beyond this place of wrath and tears
    Looms but the horror of the shade,
And yet the menace of the years
    Finds, and shall find me, unafraid.

It matters not how strait the gate,
    How charged with punishments the scroll,
I am the master of my fate,
    I am the captain of my soul.

—William Ernest Henley

Over the summer, Peter grew a few inches; that fall he lost weight, and started lifting weights. He began to feel better about his body. He found he could do his schoolwork more easily and, by the end of the first quarter, he got on the honor roll and stayed there. But, Jay claims, ever after that night Peter and Hayat seemed to have a special warmth between them. Michael has described Hayat as the queen of staff members. For Peter, she surely was.

The Rumble

Edwin, Peter and Denzel were on the Lower Merion cheerleading team. As the three of them got off the late school bus about five-thirty one November evening, they saw Denzel's cheerleading stunt partner, standing on the grass just across the street from the ABC House. We'll call her Sparkle in honor of her personality. As Edwin tells the story, "a tall guy, about eighteen, was with her. It looked as if they were slap boxing. Sparkle is small, but she's strong. She can hold her own. All of a sudden we saw the fight was turning serious, into real fists. The guy picked her up and threw her into the street. He grabbed her hair, started punching her in the face.

"We dropped our book bags and raced up to her, and the dude bounced." The attacker retreated, joining another youth and two girls who were standing watching from near the corner. Those four left and walked down Spring Avenue.

"We helped Sparkle up. She was upset and really angry." She told them that one of the girls, whom we'll call Josette, was her enemy, and had brought her boyfriend to beat Sparkle up. She wanted to go home and called her brother on her cell phone. Edwin told him, "Don't worry about it. We're going to take her home."

"As we were walking along Spring Avenue, Sparkle suddenly ran down what we thought was an alley, maybe a short cut. But it was a driveway to a bunch of townhouses. Josette and her boyfriend were there with a few others. Sparkle's brother and her mother had showed up, too. We realized Sparkle intended to continue the fight and we had walked into it. We thought, what are we doing here?

"All of a sudden, Sparkle's brother ran up to Josette's boyfriend and the other guy and started hitting them. Then they were beating him. Her brother is my friend, so I jumped in. I wasn't going to let him be in it on his own. It was two against two, and I yelled, 'Yo, Peter, hey, Denzel.' They jumped in, too. We had those guys on the ground. Then those dudes jumped up and ran into a house. It turned out to be Josette's house. Sparkle was on the porch of the same house hitting Josette and the other girl.

"Someone must have called the police. We were picking up our book bags to go when [Edwin made siren sounds here] six police cars pulled up. The cops yelled, 'Get down! Everybody down.'

"I said, 'Come on. Chill. It's not our fault.' But a cop pulled out his gun. We all hit the ground."

Denzel added, "Even all the bystanders ended up on the ground."

Edwin continued, "After Sparkle's mother explained to the police what had happened, they let us go without even taking our names. By this time we were late for dinner. We ran home, but decided not to say anything to the staff about what had happened. Why ask for trouble?

"We thought everything was cool, but later, during study hall, Josette's father showed up." One of the staff tutors answered the door and talked to him. He threatened to press charges, saying the fight had been on his property. Soon Edwin, Peter and Denzel were fielding a lot of questions from the tutor. Eventually, one of the staff called a board member, Stew Keener, then in charge of the house relations committee; he called Rob Howard, then chair of the executive committee. By the time they both arrived at the ABC House it was late in the evening.

I imagine that for Rob this must have been a nightmare. Of course, the board feels responsible for the safety of the boys in the program. On top of this, we were smack in the middle of the fall fundraising campaign, needing to raise about $110,000 in the community. A month or two earlier, our thirtieth reunion celebration had generated a host of positive news stories in the local press. What might a local newspaper make of a story about ABC students being involved in a fight that led to the police being called?

Rob and Stew convened a house meeting with all the students and staff at eleven-thirty that night, a half hour past curfew. Boys tumbled down the staircase to the first floor, some fuzzy-eyed, snatched from the first whisper of sleep, others interrupted from listening to music, or talking to roommates. They slouched on the green couches that ringed three walls of the living room, or on the giant, blue beanbag, or sprawled on the floor.

At the time, Stew was an options trader, but he had once been a staff member at another ABC House. Trying to get the story straight, Stew asked a lot of questions. In contrast, the boys recall that Rob was so upset that he kept lecturing them about giving the program a bad name. "He wouldn't listen to us," Denzel said.

The five other students: Elvis, Michael, Anthony, Jonathan and Joss, stood up for the three who were in trouble. Elvis and Michael, the two seniors and recognized house leaders, defended them strongly, saying that their behavior would be the normal response at home. They would have done the same thing. Rescuing a girl is important, honorable. And one must come to the aid of a friend. One staff tutor also stood up for them. The boys thought this was because she came from a neighborhood more like some of theirs.

Eventually, Rob and Stew told the boys that it was good that they had come to Sparkle's rescue, but they should not have escorted her home. They should have contacted her family and let them take care of her.

The house meeting lasted until twelve-thirty in the morning. After the other five students and staff members went to bed, Stew stayed and talked with the three boys for more than an hour. Meanwhile, Rob went to the police station. He was told that the program had a good reputation in the community, and that Josette and Sparkle were known for getting into fights. The police had responded to calls about them several times before. No charges would be filed against the ABC boys.

Rob and Stew and the staff agreed not to punish the boys, telling them they hoped and believed the three of them had learned a lesson about how to handle difficult situations.

The three boys told me that this would not be considered a big rumble at home. At home it could turn much more dangerous if someone had a knife or a gun. What the boys had not seen before was a girl getting beaten up. Seeing that, Edwin said, "just made us blow up inside."

Months later Rob, who grew up on the Main Line, still seemed upset about this incident. However, Edwin, Peter and Denzel, who had seen themselves as heroes—knights in sweatshirts and oversized jeans—just wanted to put it behind them. But Peter said wistfully, "Sometimes people don't see the good things we do."

Tyrell's Commentary: A Fair Fight

Tyrell, who had graduated a few years earlier, offered these comments when he read this story: "I would have acted the same way and walked the girl home. I'd have left when her mother and brother were there. They wouldn't need me anymore because her family was there."

But when Edwin's friend was in trouble, "Edwin did what he was supposed to do. You're not supposed to stand there when your friend is being jumped. I would have reacted the same way. But Peter and Denzel shouldn't have jumped in. Two on two is a fair fight. If anything, they could have tried to break it up instead of jumping in. Even now if kids on my block are going to fight, I am going to make sure it is a fair fight. I'm twenty years old, one of the oldest. Everyone respects me. It's not going to be five on one or two on one. I'm going to make sure it is fair.

"In my neighborhood [in Brooklyn] when I was growing up, you got into a problem, you would fight right then and there, and then that would be it. With Edwin and Peter and Denzel that's the same thing. Since the police didn't even keep them, they were off the hook. That's why they didn't want to say anything. What's done is done."

The Black Path

Late one weekend evening, Hayat was heading to her rooms on the third floor when, from the second floor landing, she heard female voices floating out of Peter's room. Suddenly, his door flew open and Peter stood in the doorway. In a flash the door slammed shut again.

Hayat strode to the door and knocked. Peter, looking sheepish, opened it. She saw what looked like a tea party laid out, Kool-Aid and cookies, and the backs of girls disappearing onto the fire escape. Stammering, Peter, who at the time was a freshman, told her that one of the girls was upset and needed to talk to a friend. Peter was acting as that friend. Yes, he knew he wasn't supposed to have girls up to his room. He was sorry.

The next day Hayat contacted the chair of the house relations committee and they meted out Peter's punishment: grounding for a weekend or two. It would seem that the incident was behind him, but Peter was branded as the guy brazen enough, even as a freshman, to sneak girls into his room.

Three years later, Peter startled Jay and me when we asked him about this incident. "I was just being a host," he said.

"Yeah, you were entertaining the girls," I said.

"No, I was being a host." He said that the girls were coming to see two upperclassmen, but it was easier to sneak up the fire escape to Peter's room.

"But you had the Kool-Aid and cookies," I said.

"I said I was being a host. Their room was messy so they wanted to use my room." He went on to say that the girls were late arriving and he had fallen asleep. He awoke, disoriented, when they came in the fire escape door. He wondered what these people were doing in his room. He jumped up and opened his door to the hallway when Hayat happened to be going by at just that moment. He made up the story about why the girls were there. "I wasn't going to snitch. It's the code. I was a freshman trying to hang out with older guys."

"Didn't the older boys come to your aid when you got in trouble?" I asked.

"No, Sam wasn't going to do that. He told me, 'They won't kick you out. I've gotten into lots more trouble and they haven't kicked me out.'"

This incident was just one of many troubles Peter had his first year at ABC. Stress nearly smothered him. Along with all the problems he was having adjusting to being at ABC, he believed he was fat and hated the way he looked. At some point in the winter, he decided the way to slim down was to force himself to throw up. At first it was hard to do, but soon it got much easier and the pounds slid off.

One night Elvis heard him throwing up, marched into the bathroom and told him to stop doing it. However, Peter didn't stop. After a couple of weeks he found not only was it easy to throw up, but he was throwing up even when he didn't intend to. Feeling weak and woozy, he confided in Michael, who sought Jay out.

Hayat and her husband Frank rushed to the store and bought ginger ale for him to drink, and she called a board member who was a physician. They discussed hospitalizing him that night, but elected to see if the fluids improved how he felt. The next day Peter saw a doctor who put him on Pedialyte. After that scare, Peter stopped making himself vomit, but the staff worried about it for the rest of the year, and again the next year when he joined the school's wrestling team.

Peter was much happier his second year. He had adjusted to school, lost some weight, but best of all, he now had two compatriots: Anthony and Edwin.

That spring, board member Wes Bradley helped Peter get a summer internship through ABC National. Peter worked at USB Bank, lived with relatives in New York, and came back with more self-confidence.

That fall, as a junior, he joined the cheerleading team along with Edwin and a freshman, Denzel. He was earning quite good grades. One problem had risen over the summer: Peter had picked up smoking from some of his relatives. Since our rules forbid smoking, he tried to hide it by smoking on the fire escape, and then flushing the butts down the toilet.

At the start of his junior year Peter read a poem he had written for the poetry event at the thirtieth reunion celebration. Here is part of the poem.

The Black Path

On a long gaping black path leading to all damnation
You refuse to believe it; you think it's all a hallucination
Refuse to accept the consequences for your actions
But, in the end you must realize you're liable for termination
To all those who decide your fate you are a mere fraction
You must realize that it was you who brought it upon yourself,
    the whole condemnation.
Your hubris pride and arrogant attitude sent you to a point in the
Black path of no return, where you cannot turn back . . .
When you are lost forever, you hear a voice whispering o' so
    beautiful words,
"Don't worry my child you will be all right, you will
be given a second chance, but beware because there might not
be a thrice."

The poem proved to be prescient.

One January afternoon, Monica, that year's resident director, came home from work early. Walking into the living room, she spied a girl's purse. When she questioned Jonathan and Joss, who were freshmen, about the purse, they told her it belonged to Peter's girlfriend. Monica asked where they were.

"Ah, they went for a walk," Joss said as Jonathan headed for the stairs.

"Sit down!" Monica ordered as she started up the stairs.

When Peter answered her knock, he was clad in only his boxer shorts. Yawning, stretching, he told her he'd been taking a nap. Monica walked in, crossed the room, and opened the closet door. There stood girlfriend.

A couple of nights later, several board members gathered in the house office to discuss how to deal with this. Peter told us later that he sat in his room feeling scared. "Each person came up to yell at me because it was so stupid. They said, 'You've been back and forth to the edge; you've been testing our patience. We don't know if you are even going to be here by the end of the week.' My academic advisor called me a con artist and it felt like crap.

"I called my mom and I said, 'I'm coming home.' My Mom wasn't mad at me. She said I was stupid! She didn't see what I did as too bad.

"When they [board members] met with me they warned me this was the meeting where they would decide whether or not I got kicked out. Monica came up to my room crying, 'Peter, why do you always have to put yourself in situations like you're trying to get kicked out.' I didn't do anything to hurt anybody. In October of that year they found out I was smoking and then in November we had that big old fight [the Rumble]." Apparently, several members of the house relations committee wanted to kick Peter out, feeling that this kid was just too high maintenance. Among the issues board members raised, a serious one was that of risk for the ABC program. If a girl got pregnant or charged rape, the program, which relied on good will and donations from the community, could be sunk. Peter was now a two-time offender for having girls in his room. Incorrigible.

The executive committee called an emergency meeting of the full board, a necessary step before removing a student from the program. Although the house relations committee, with one or two dissensions, recommended he be sent home permanently, a majority of the board members voted no. Instead the board decided that he had to leave the cheerleading team, do a community service activity after school several days a week, and be under the close supervision of an ad hoc committee.

Peter stayed. He volunteered after school at an assisted living home where he helped with activities and meals, and became quite popular with many of the residents.

I volunteered, along with five other board members, to be on the oversight committee, or, as we dubbed it, the Peter Rescue Squad. In addition to providing rides to his service activity, we crowded into the cluttered, stuffy staff office once a week, listened to a staff member's report, discussed what we should talk to him about that week, and then called Peter in. We tried hard to praise him for what he was doing well, before discussing any current problems. As a group we were functioning as "parents" of a boy who alternately tried to fulfill the requirements set out for him, and chafed mightily against them.

The biggest drama centered on his girlfriend's senior prom. We decided he was doing well enough to go to the prom. But Peter also wanted to go to an after-prom party in the neighborhood. We said no. His backup proposal was to sleep over at a male friend's house. No. At that discussion, Peter sat rooted in his chair saying nothing, then suddenly jumped up, raced out of the room and slammed the door so hard that the glass pane quivered.

In a minute a staff member, having heard the slam, rushed in. "What happened?" We reassured him everything was okay; Peter was just being a teenager.

Our concern was how to ensure that Peter returned to the ABC House as soon as the prom ended. We didn't trust him when he said he'd come home with a friend from the neighborhood. And we didn't trust him not to get into trouble if he stayed out all night. Wes Bradley volunteered to pick up Peter and his date at the prom and drive them home. Well, that would be like having your father pick you up!

Finally, Elvis came to his rescue. He offered to take responsibility for seeing that Peter came home right after the prom. We told Elvis he didn't have to do this; after all, this was his senior prom. He insisted he didn't mind. Since everyone on the committee trusted Elvis to do what he said he would, we settled on that. Peter went off to the prom in a state of high excitement and came back to the ABC House on time.

Our second big worry centered on his plans for the summer. Peter had again secured an attractive internship, this time with J.P. Morgan Chase in New York City. His parents lived in Hartford. For Peter to live with the relatives he had stayed with the summer before was not an option. This time it was Elvis's mother who came to the rescue, agreeing to let him live with her family.

At the end of the school year, Peter had good grades and had stayed out of major trouble—although he had had a number of skirmishes with our committee. The executive board decided that our Peter Rescue Committee should disband, and Peter would just be supervised by the staff and the house relations committee, the same as all the other students. We on Peter's committee were left with a mixture of hope and trepidation. Even though he was doing pretty well in keeping out of trouble, he had a well-trod "Black Path." Wes, who was on both the executive board and the oversight committee, told Peter they were not giving him any slack; he was to stay on the straight and narrow. The six of us knew that if he should have another major infraction, we would not be able to save him.

Peter later summed up where he was at that point: "I was in the program, I was out of restrictions and I was a senior. I felt like I came out on top."

The End of the Line

Fat Tuesday, a chilly February night. Three figures stole softly down the fire escape on the south side of the house. That side of the house was covered in darkness—it was after the eleven o'clock, in-your-room curfew. The three members of the LLES (Latin Lovers Escort Service), Anthony, Peter and Edwin, were almost to the last rung of the last ladder, Edwin in the lead. Friends were waiting in a car across the street to take them to a dance club in the city for Mardi Gras.

Out of the darkness, a voice: "Stop right there!"

Peter told me, "I thought, Oh, crap! Now I'm really in for it." The voice belonged to Laurie (not her real name), one of the resident directors.

The three jumped down the rest of the ladder and raced around the front of the house. Edwin, whose room was on the far side, had left the door to the fire escape from his room unlocked. Maybe they could get back there before anyone figured out who they were.

They rounded the corner to the driveway. Just as they were starting up the fire escape to Edwin's room, they saw Dean, the other resident director, standing against the edge of the house. He stepped out of the shadows.

"Stop!" he said. Anthony and Peter gave up but Edwin scampered up the fire escape and stepped into his room. There he threw off his clothes, rumpled up his hair, and popped into bed.

Anthony and Peter went into the house with Dean. Peter recalls, "Anthony and I thought, damn! This has never happened before." Dean told Anthony to go get Edwin. When Edwin came down he was in his boxer shorts and socks and was stretching, feigning sleepiness. Dean said, "Don't even try."

Peter told us, "I thought, this is a trap. It was just after eleven. They are usually inside cleaning up. But they were outside, waiting for us.

"Dean had us clean up the kitchen first, really clean up the kitchen. Then he sat us in the living room. Sat us in three different spots and told us to write down where we were going. Because it was a weeknight we had our stories prepared. Edwin and I said we were buying birthday cards for a girl. Anthony said he was buying something else. Going to Rite Aid is what we usually do on a weeknight [if they sneak out]."

Peter went on: "Dean said he was very disappointed in Anthony because Anthony never does anything bad. He was very disappointed in Edwin. When he came to me he said, 'I don't even know what to say to you anymore.' He said 'You brought Anthony and Edwin into this!' I was like, 'I didn't bring anybody into anything. This was just the first time we all got caught together.'

"The next night when they [the house relations committee] had their meeting, Edwin and Anthony got their punishments"—grounding for a weekend. "They were called in first. I was the last one. I kept saying to myself, 'I'm screwed.' They came up to me and said, 'We're not ready for you.'

"I knew I was getting removed."

When he reflected back on the incident, Peter first thought one of the boys in the house had given them away, but later he remembered, "I was hitting on one of the Haverford students" who volunteered as an occasional tutor at the house. He told her what they were planning, and he thinks Laurie overheard them. Jonathan heard her go back to Dean and say, "Something's going down tonight."

About the year up until then, Peter said, "As usual, I had a good first quarter. I always do. I was trying to be a positive influence and lead the younger kids in a positive direction. I knew they were going to look up to me since I was a senior. I don't know how the staff felt, but I was trying to be a leader."

In February Peter had had a week of cascading troubles. He had an altercation with a staff member who thought he was playing his music too loudly in his room. Then on a Saturday during weekly room check, the staff tutor who was on duty found a cigarette butt in his toilet. Peter told me, "I thought, crap! And I thought I flushed that thing." Then came Fat Tuesday.

The house relations committee and executive board met and recommended removing him from the program. Rob Howard, executive committee chair, called an emergency meeting for the next Saturday morning. He asked that the staff and all of the students leave the house so that no one would overhear our discussion. Almost the entire membership of the board showed up. We filled up all the chairs at the long dining room table. Extra chairs were dragged in, but still one person sat on the radiator, another perched on the buffet, and others stood along the back wall or leaned against doorjambs.

I felt heartsick. Peter was in the second semester of his senior year, had a strong GPA, and was waiting to hear from colleges.

Rob opened the meeting by summarizing the charges. In addition to Peter's troubles the previous week, there had been a couple of incidents after Thanksgiving break. Those of us who had been on the Peter Rescue Squad the previous spring had come to understand that the same traits that got Peter into trouble with us, were survival skills for him in his home setting. Every time he came back from home, he had to readjust his behavior. Added to that, he was an impulsive boy who was used to lying to cover up when he got caught.

No one at the meeting knew yet that the three boys had been sneaking out for Mardi Gras. That didn't matter. The critical factor, as Rob said, was that "The staff is tired of dealing with him." For me that was the pivotal point as well. Our staff members were all young adults in graduate school or with day jobs. Their jobs with us were hard: living with, supervising, and mentoring a whole houseful of teenaged boys. They had struggled to support and deal with Peter's ups and downs. Now their hourglass of patience with him had run out.

After a considerable discussion, the board voted to remove him from the program. However, several of us were very concerned about his being able to make it to graduation, only a few months away. Lisa Kahn, a new board member, volunteered to let him stay at her house until a suitable place could be found for him. That night Peter moved in with the Kahns for two weeks.

You Miss Them When They're Gone

To stay in our program, students must maintain a minimum grade point average of 2.8, and stay within the bounds of house rules. From time to time a student does not manage to do one or both of these and is not "invited back," as we euphemistically term it, or occasionally is even removed mid-year— as in Peter's case.

When Jay and I talked with the students, we found a sizeable disconnect between how the board and the students perceive this situation. The board meetings where we consider removing a student are usually fraught with tension, often with disagreements and certainly with sorrow. We are always focused on the individual student, and on the staff's reports regarding the problems the student is causing in the house and for the staff.

When we consider the effect of removing a student, we imagine that his absence will be a boon by removing someone who consumes a disproportionate amount of the staff's attention and energy, and who is setting a bad example either academically, in their actions or both. A year before Peter was removed from the program, Jay and I had a hypothetical discussion about this with Michael and Elvis.

Michael said, "I've never heard a student say they want [another] student kicked out. There are times when they deserve to be kicked out, but I don't think we want that."

The students figure out that something is going on when board members start coming over to the house for meetings, and closeting themselves with the resident director in the office for hours. At some point the student in trouble is called in to meet with the adults. Usually, the student's parent or parents are asked to come from their home out of state to meet with the executive board and the chair of the appropriate committee: academic or house relations.

The goal of the meeting is to work out a process and provide supports to enable the student to stay in the program and to enlist the parents' aid in this. Sometimes it works; often it does not. For example, when Tom (not his real name), who was in the class ahead of Elvis and Michael, was in his junior year, his grades were below the required GPA. A handful of members of the board's academic committee—including me—took turns during the spring semester, meeting with him once a week along with one of the staff tutors. We could not figure out why he was doing so poorly, and he didn't seem as motivated to improve his grades as we were to have him do so. We warned him many times that he might be dismissed if he didn't show improvement. Still, he was reportedly shocked the following summer when he was told that he could not come back for his senior year.

I asked Michael and Elvis, "When you see these meetings going on, are you worried about it?"

Michael said, "Yeah, I feel anxious to know what is going to happen. As an older guy I try to help them out. Keep them clean."

Elvis joined in, saying, "I really feel bad. You get to thinking you don't want anyone in this program to ever get kicked out. Even if I don't like the student, once they're gone, you just miss them."

To our surprise, Michael added, "Every single student who is kicked out keeps in contact. For months afterwards, Ned would call us. I still talk to Tom; I still talk to Earl [not his real name]. I wish more people could hear Tom say, he wishes he had worked harder. It's not easy after being kicked out. He wishes he were still here."

The boys have many ways of keeping in contact including visits when they are home on break.

While the conversation with Elvis and Michael was a general one, I later talked to Anthony and Edwin individually about what happened in the house when Peter was removed from ABC. Anthony said, "The night Rob told Peter he was getting kicked out, I didn't know what to do. Edwin and I went to his room and talked for about a half hour. I felt very bad. We all cried that night. Edwin and I looked up to him because he had been in the program longer."

The day Peter came to move his things out of the house, Anthony was away and Edwin was the only one of the boys who helped Peter move. Edwin tried to give him a picture of them together in Times Square that was taken when Peter visited him during one Christmas break. They only had one copy between them. Peter started bawling. Edwin said, "Peter told me 'No, you keep it.' That broke my heart.

"We talked that night. We talked every night."

I asked if he saw him at school. "Every day. I made sure I saw him. He's my friend! Even though the staff didn't want me to hang out with him after school, I still hung out with him. How could I not?"

While Anthony usually came home within an hour or so after school, now he didn't come until dinnertime because Peter wasn't there. He could see him at school, but Peter was not allowed at the house.

Edwin said, "It was just a different place without him."

What eased their pain somewhat was the concern of Tim, a staff tutor who reached out to them. Anthony said, "Tim offered these cool events, like going to plays. Edwin and I were the only ones who went with him."

One evening Tim took Anthony and Edwin to the Jersey Shore. Anthony said, "We sat on the beach in the dark. We had so much fun! It was one of the best times I ever had. It made it much easier."

Peter, meanwhile, faced lots of challenges—finding a place to live, earning money, and getting into college if he still could.

CHAPTER 8

The Personal Consequences of Success

The ABC program is designed to change lives. But in enabling disadvantaged youth to vault into the educated middle class, the program also forces these students to grapple with disconnections from their families and their cultures, and the different mores and expectations of their new environment. These struggles only compound the normal "Who am I?" searching so typical of teenagers.

Tyrell had never been away from home before he came to us as a freshman. The first night, he slept better than he expected to. The first week, he called home every single day. After that he talked to his parents every week all through his four years at ABC. He might talk with them for twenty minutes, but often it didn't seem enough. Yet he said he never really felt homesick. He thought this was because he comes from a big family and there were always people around at ABC so it didn't seem strange. "There was always somebody to talk to."

I asked him if he felt as if he was losing touch with his siblings.

"I didn't notice that in high school, but now when I'm in college I do. When I'm home in the summer and everybody's in the kitchen and they are talking about a situation that happened and I'm looking around and they say, 'Oh, you weren't here.' My brother-in-law said, 'It's like you don't live here. You just visit a lot.'

"I left at fourteen and I grew up in the ABC program. My mom raised me but she didn't see me grow up."

Although Tyrell clearly has some regret over what he missed with his family, to whom he remains very close, in his usual accepting way he said, "There's not really much you can do about it. It's one of the consequences. You just have to go with the punches."

Jonathan and Elvis both felt more uncomfortable about how being at ABC had affected how they related to their families. By his senior year, Jonathan was the only native Spanish-speaking student in the ABC House, and had nobody to speak it with. "I feel lonely. I don't have anyone to relate to with the same skin color, either." He was quite busy keeping up with a demanding course load, taking part in school clubs, acting in a school play, singing in the school choir, applying to selective colleges and being a respected house leader for the younger boys in the house. Board and staff members regarded him as one of our prize success stories. Yet, toward the end of that year, he wrote an essay for his senior English class, excerpted here.

Sometimes I feel like I am not good enough for my family. When I go back home I feel like that because ever since I left for the ABC program, my family says I am not Puerto Rican enough. Despite what I do to make my family happy, they say that I am starting to act white . . .

What does it mean to be Puerto Rican anyway? Is it eating *arroz con abichuelas y chuletas* every day? Is it talking Spanish with your family? If that is the case, I do that all the time. Does my family feel like I am trying to be better than they are because I want to pursue higher education? I still have all the values that have been set in me by both of my parents and everyone else in my family. I have not abandoned my heritage or nationality in any way. As a matter of fact, I have a huge Puerto Rican flag hanging up on my bedroom wall right now . . . They feel like I have molded into a typical white kid from the suburbs. The reason why they think so is because I talk differently and I have dissimilar beliefs that contradict my traditional culture.

In his essay, Jonathan also brought up how he had learned at ABC to handle conflict differently from the way his family does.

My mom and my brother get angry very easily when it comes to certain issues, whereas, I am calm and I think about situations and try to talk them out . . . At home, I try to change the way my family handles situations because at ABC, we talk about our issues and learn to solve them without having to be disrespectful . . . Maybe I have changed, but to become a better person. My family, however, makes it seem like the change is negative . . .

I have asked my brothers what they see differently about me. They say I talk, dress and act differently . . . They say it as if they are ashamed of me, and I feel like I am no longer part of the family, like they think I am from another family, a white family. This past summer, my brother Jimmy said to me after I went jogging, "Jon, why do you run? Are you white all of a sudden?"

Jonathan wrote that he felt the people where he lived then (the people at ABC) accepted him for who he is. Why can't his family? "I know who I am, I know where I was born, and I can never forget that."

Elvis also struggled with how being at ABC affected his place in his family. In his junior year he wrote the following essay, "How to Tell them in Words," for his honors English class.

Not living in Brooklyn brought me to an ideological conflict between who I am, and who my family would have made me had

I stayed home. Staying home means the constant speeches of my father. His favorite words are, "be a leader, not a follower." Then again there is the occasional, "don't give your heart to a woman." My dad might use the two interchangeably, even when such words have no relevance to my problems, but I know he means well. My mother's advice is "You always do the opposite of what your father says." I just try to block them both out and do the best I can in life, and, of course, both parents take full credit for me being the good boy of the family.

Somewhere between the three years I have been at this program, I am no longer my mother's good son. Her once correct and unquestioning words are now replied with doubtful, almost mockingly questioning. How could she say such things I ask. My mother takes this as my not being her good little boy. A respectful Spanish boy does not disrespect his mother, but he takes her insults with his head down. American parents make their children look them in the eye, but my mother understands that to be a challenge to her respect. If I look up at those fiery eyes when she speaks, it's like my going in for the attack, and my mother receives a jolt of fear that I am actually going against her. She cries saying, when they grow up they lose their respect. I never meant to be bad to my mother.

I really looked up to my father; but when my parents fought, my dad was always the bad guy. My mother came crying and telling us children that our father puts a price on us and didn't want to give her money for our school clothes. This is what I know to be a Spanish man's burden. My dad was always too poor to have what he wanted as a child, so he still yearns for some material possessions as a man but does not have the money to afford such because he has to provide for his children. Solution, drinking. Drinking solved the problem of the nagging wife you couldn't leave, the disrespectful step-daughter who acts as though you have no authority over her because you are not her REAL father, and maintaining the macho ideals of a man.

My dad leads a miserable life, and he vents toward me his frustration and failures as a man. Despite all his shortcomings, I admired my father. As a child I dreamt of the day I'd grow up, being the man my family wanted me to be, and drinking a Bud with my dad while he is flying his pigeons. Today I am closer to being a man than I have ever been, and it is my dad who I can relate to. My mom made fun of my dad once for having no friends and that being the reason my dad made me work at the hot dog stand with him. But isn't that the relationship a man should have with his son?

Now over a hundred miles away, my parents know less and less of who I am becoming and I don't know how to tell them in words because I am just finding out. I find myself more and more not relating to people of the society I come from; I just view so many of them as ignorant. My brother thinks this is because I am arrogant, or a sell out.

In another essay for the same class, Elvis wrote that his mother didn't want him to do manual labor or any kind of work that involved using his hands. She felt he had been given a great mind and one day would grow up and hold a job, one "that only requires me to think." His mother did not want his father to teach him about fixing things such as cars or house repairs. But, Elvis wrote, "I like doing work with my hands. I like breaking a sweat, and I like getting dirty while working. I feel so satisfied after I complete a strenuous job because I can say I accomplished something."

For his senior experience project Elvis crafted several beautiful pieces of pottery at the local community art center. He paid for his time there by helping to build a kiln.

He had come to ABC thinking he wanted to be a doctor, but those dreams beached on the shoals of an honors chemistry class. Because he liked to write and got rewards for doing so, he toyed with the idea of becoming an English teacher—

not just an English teacher, but one teaching in inner-city Brooklyn where he had grown up. For his last poetry event as a senior he recited, with considerable verve, a poem inspired by his mother's reaction to this.

Poor Mamma

I told my mom I wanted to help the poor
So now I am a disappointment.
All my life:
My son is a good little boy,
He gonna be a lawyer or a judge,
Gonna be the reason your kids get out of prison.
And he gonna be rich,
Rich, rich, rich,
Gonna buy me a house and put his daddy in a nursing home
Because once my son is supporting me,
I won't be needing him.

But now he ruins my life, Not gonna be rich,
Boy, don't you ruin my life.
RUIN your Own,
But once I am dead.
You supposed to make me rich,
Make me forget about my times
On Welfare, collecting food stamps, using Medicaids, and
    depending on Section Eight to pay my rent.

Do you love your mother . . . I guess not.
Want to help the streets,
Boy, if the streets gave you so much why'd you leave Brooklyn?
Let me think,
Is a Jacuzzi too much to ask for?
It's the least you could do for me

CHAPTER 9

Moving On

Charles: Next Step—The Ivy League

Unlike Tyrell, Charles's basketball career did not end with high school graduation. The boy who came to us from automotive school was accepted to an Ivy League university, and played on their team for two of his four college years.

While Charles had not felt stereotyped as a black student when he was at Lower Merion, he did feel somewhat that way at college. He found that most of the black and Latino students lived on one part of campus. Also, "White frat students will [sometimes] yell derogatory things."

He majored in philosophy and, once again, often found himself the only black student in class. But now it was less stressful for him because he felt people understood that when he said something, it was just his own opinion, and not representing his whole race.

Tyrell and a Couple of Fairy Godmothers

The central mission of our ABC program is to prepare students for college and to help them get there. As any parent who has helped a child through the college application process knows, this is a time-and-emotion-consuming activity. The difference is that the ABC boys rely on a whole bunch of people to help them through the process. Tyrell's story illustrates how it goes.

Tyrell didn't believe in fairy godmothers, but when he needed one, not one, but two, showed up: Lois and Kay. Lois appeared early in his life at ABC. In the first few months of his freshman year Tyrell got into trouble. He could have been kicked out of the program, but the executive board decided to give him another chance. Lois Davis, a retired assistant U.S. Attorney, was on the executive board at the time and became his mother hen. She told him, "Everyone is entitled to one mistake. You had the misfortune to make yours the first quarter of your first year. You have to be clean from now on." And he was.

Tyrell was on the high school honor roll for most of his time at ABC but, by the spring of his junior year, he was feeling stressed. The college process had started, and there was so much to do. Our ABC program pays to have SAT tutoring for our students starting in the winter and spring of their junior year. Tyrell was the only junior that year, so he alone had to do the extra studying for the SAT tests.

Then he needed to develop a list of colleges. Jim Nolan, a private college guidance counselor, worked with our ABC students for many years pro bono. Tyrell started meeting with him that spring and into the fall, exploring what type of college he'd like to attend, and then researching a long list of colleges that Jim suggested.

In addition to meeting with Jim, Tyrell met some evenings with Marnie Christian, who was then in charge of college guidance for our ABC program. They talked about the list of schools Jim was helping him develop, and explored ideas for the essays he would need to write the next fall for his applications.

Basketball season was particularly tough on Tyrell that year, since he was playing JV, but he also was second string on the varsity team. That meant that he had to double up on practices. He spent more time at practice, for example, than Charles did—and Charles was a star of the varsity team. Tyrell loved playing basketball, but it took much time and energy. Practice and games frequently made him late for study hall or made him miss it altogether. Tyrell tried to make up the time doing homework after school or late at night, but he didn't always get all of his work done.

And that meant he had to deal with Mary Storey and me, who together were supervising the academic program for the board. We had always been supportive, praising him for how well he performed at school. Now we constantly asked him if he was really keeping up on his homework, and reminded him how important his junior year grades were. For Tyrell, we had turned into nags.

To make it all worse, since Tyrell was the only junior that year, nobody else in the house was sharing this pressure. His best buddy, Charles, already knew he'd be going to an Ivy League university. Charles was feeling relaxed. So relaxed, in fact, that he was gripped by a bad case of senioritis.

By the time of the annual poetry night in April, Tyrell was feeling put upon, so put upon. For the event he wrote a poem he called "Why?" The gist of it was: "Why are you always on my back?" Writing it made him feel that at least he wasn't taking it all lying down.

Tyrell found senior year easier because he only had to make out the applications, write his essays and wait to hear back. He felt in good hands with Marnie, and was hopeful of getting into some good schools and receiving decent aid packages. After all his applications were mailed, he relaxed and concentrated on enjoying his last, wonderful season of basketball.

Spring came, and with spring came letters from colleges. Several schools accepted him, including his first choice: Syracuse University. The only problem: the aid package from Syracuse was not quite big enough. Marnie worked on trying to improve it.

Re-enter fairy godmother number one. One day that spring, Lois found herself sitting next to Kay Lovelace Taylor at a meeting of Links, an African American women's service club. Kay had been an executive in the Philadelphia School District and now was teaching at Temple University. Her husband, H. Le Baron Taylor, a vice president of Sony, had died recently. Kay mentioned to Lois that she was setting up a college scholarship in her husband's memory to be given to a student of color. It would be worth ten thousand dollars for one year.

"Ah, do I have a student for you," Lois said and told her about Tyrell. Kay agreed to consider him, but first, she wanted to meet him.

They agreed to meet at the ABC House one afternoon after school. Lois arrived early to coach Tyrell on how to present himself. Tyrell, who had been raised as one of five children in a well-structured home, was an unfailingly courteous young man, so Lois probably felt confident it would go all right. When Kay arrived she told Tyrell she didn't have any set procedure in mind—did he have a suggestion?

"Let's go for a walk," he told her.

They started down the street, talking as they went. They had not yet made it all of the way around the block when Kay said, "You've got it."

Within a few days Marnie and Mary Storey saw a problem. Tyrell didn't need ten thousand for his first year; that much would cut into his aid package and he would lose part of it. What he needed was a smaller amount spread over all four years. Lois talked Kay into rethinking how she gave the money. He would get twenty-five hundred for each of four years.

Kay planned to make the presentation of the award at the annual meeting of the Boulé (Sigma Pi Phi), an organization of black professionals, to be held in New Orleans in late June. She promised she would pay for airfare and lodging for Tyrell to come, but she needed a photo of him for the brochure that would accompany the award. Lois's husband took a photo of Tyrell. Since Tyrell did not own a tailored jacket, in the photo he was wearing a sweatshirt. Soon Kay let Lois know, emphatically, that this was not the image she had in mind.

Time was running out when Curt Wilson, former president of the ABCLM board and an excellent amateur photographer, came over to the house one evening to take another picture. All the men in the house rushed around bringing out jackets for Tyrell to try on. He was six-foot-one or so and skinny; none of the jackets fit. Curt was easily the nattiest dresser on the board, and now off came his impeccably tailored jacket. The sleeves ended midway down Tyrell's arms. Not to worry, Curt told him, we only need your shoulders for the shot.

That would do for the brochure, but what about the award ceremony itself? The ABC executive board decided that the program should outfit him, and fortunately, the fund drive had come in over budget that year. One spring evening Wes Bradley took Tyrell shopping for a suit, shirt, belt, dress shoes and tie. A few weeks after school was out, Tyrell flew to New Orleans for the presentation. Later Kay told Lois that she was very pleased with his speech at the ceremony—and with his appearance.

Two years later, just before starting his junior year at Syracuse where he was majoring in management studies and finance, Tyrell told me, "Without the Taylor scholarship, I could never have gone to Syracuse."

Applying to college was not the only stress in Tyrell's life that year. His father, who had accompanied him on his first visit to Ardmore, was the major adult presence in his life. Jay and other staff members recall that, whenever they called his parents to update them about Tyrell, his parents had already heard the news from Tyrell during the long phone conversations they had every week. Now his father's diabetes had progressed to the point that he was on dialysis three times a week, and could no longer work. At the annual poetry reading in April of his senior year, Tyrell read the following poem he wrote for his father.

What is a Man?

What is a MAN?
Does being a MAN have to do with becoming a certain age?
No. There's much more to manhood than age.
Being a MAN is about taking care of responsibilities.
No MAN would leave the mother of his kids by herself,
Or run away from his problems.
Being a MAN is about respecting women.
No MAN would ever strike one.
Being a MAN is about sacrifice.
No Man would put his priorities before his children's.
My dad is a MAN, because he took care of his responsibilities.
He is a MAN because he respects my mom,
And he is a MAN because he always puts his kids first.
I hope one day I am half the MAN my dad is, better yet
I just hope to be a MAN.

Too ill to travel, his father missed Tyrell's high school graduation. When Tyrell traveled home from Syracuse for Thanksgiving the next fall, his father was in the hospital. Tyrell was able to visit him twice. By Christmas, the strong father, who taught his son how to be a man, was gone.

Elvis: Becoming the One Percent

The ABC House lies just a few blocks from Haverford College, and some of our students get to know the campus and college students who volunteer as tutors at the house. I don't know how Elvis came to like Haverford, but by the end of his sophomore year he was talking of wanting to go there. Early in his junior year, I went with him for the college tour. Many of the prospective students on the tour were chattering among themselves and asking a lot of questions of the guide. I sensed right away that Elvis was feeling shy and ill at ease, yet he projected a Mr. Cool image. The only time he spoke up was when the guide, a girl, made a mistake describing what division a particular sport at Haverford was in. He corrected her.

Broad-shouldered Elvis played several sports at Lower Merion, including shot put and throwing discus. On the tour, I caught several girls casting interested looks at him, but he stayed aloof. There were more girls than guys on the tour, and two skinny boys, friends from prep school, were mildly rough-housing and generally acting immature. This seemed to heighten the girls' interest in quiet Elvis.

Marnie Christian had been Elvis's academic advisor since he was a freshman and a hardworking student well liked by his teachers. They enjoyed a comfortable relationship. In an earlier job, Marnie had worked as associate admissions director at an elite college, and for several years she had helped our seniors with their college applications. She was planning to step down from our board soon, but promised to stay on long enough to help Elvis and Michael.

We normally do not encourage our students to try for early action or early decision to college. Financial aid is critical for them, and getting an early acceptance can put them at a disadvantage for negotiating aid. In addition, in the fall of their senior year our boys are usually just starting to sort out what kind of college they want to attend; but Elvis was unusually confident about what he wanted. Since Marnie thought it was reasonable for him to apply early, we all deferred to her. Elvis kept saying, "I'm counting on Marnie."

For his essay, Elvis retold a story he had read to our board when he was a sophomore about his middle school teacher, but he added a thoughtful piece about how he had felt being at Lower Merion High School. He wrote:

I remember that day so vividly. Mr. Rivera stormed into the classroom with a bit more fury than was usual for a moody person like himself. He paced over to his desk and began to lecture the class on why he had a bad mood. He said he saw some disheartening statistics on the drop out rate in a poor suburb of New York. The . . . statistic he kept preaching was the last one percent. That (only) one out of every one hundred kids in the district . . . graduated from a four-year college. Naturally, in the aura of my teacher's fury all of us looked around as he lectured us that, statistically, none of us might graduate from college . . .

It hurt Mr. Rivera to see such numbers because he dreamt that so much would become of all of us. After my acceptance to "A Better Chance" at Lower Merion, he told me that I had the best chance at being that one percent, if I kept focused. He thought getting out of Brooklyn was the best thing for me to do, second only to attending his alma mater Brooklyn Tech.

School away from home initially made me miserable, but I remained focused on my work. I did miss my family, but it was their expectation that I do well that kept me in this program. I hated that my new classmates doubted me. To them, I was another ABC guy whose purpose was to make Lower Merion sport teams better and maybe tackle one or two honors courses. I wanted so badly to prove them wrong and be recognized as the special person I was to my peers in Brooklyn.

Getting the respect of my peers on the sports fields was easy but it mattered more to me that I was respected for my mind. I got the respect I wanted while taking Mr. Segal's English class my junior year. He graded my papers harshly, and he even had a trademark skull and crossbones stamp that he stamped each of my papers at least three times. The stamp indicated that I broke one of the deadly sins of writing. I thought I was a horrible writer, but one day I allowed Mr. Segal to read a short essay I wrote. The assignment was to write to Chris McCandless as the main character in, *To Build A Fire*. I totally disagreed with Chris' idea about nature's power to soothe people's problems. I attested that

Alaska's lack of food, vastness, and dangers do not soothe people. Instead, people need every advantage they can get to live there. I ended my short essay stating that the only soothing nature gave me was the numbness of my last slumber. I saw my classmates' mouths drop, and I finally heard one of them say that I wrote something better than they did.

Afterward, I noticed such a difference in the way people in that class treated me. All of a sudden people paid close attention to what I had to contribute to the class, and even Mr. Segal looked forward to my almost daily debasing of the prior night's assigned reading. I felt like I regained the perception my peers had of me when I was in Brooklyn. People in both Brooklyn and Lower Merion now view me as an intellectual.

I now need to take the next step to be that one percent in Mr. Rivera's speech. I made a choice to leave home for a Lower Merion education, and I made a choice to go beyond my peers' expectations of me to move closer to the one percent. I made a choice to apply early decision to Haverford, because my desire to go to your school is just as strong as my desire to be that one percent.

Elvis was accepted early decision at Haverford College, and entered as a freshman in the fall of 2004. He graduated four years later.

Michael: Staying in Philadelphia

During his senior year, Michael's host parents, Rex and Meg Goldberg, helped him to fill out his college applications on host Sundays. He planned to apply to American University in Washington, D.C., and was arranging to go visit there. "I had never been to D.C. I told them I wish I'd have time to see other places. Just out of the blue they said, 'Oh, we're free that weekend. We'll meet you, spend the night in a hotel, and we'll go tour D.C.' I remember staying in the hotel and it was the nicest hotel that I'd ever been in. I thought I'd be sharing a room with them, but I had my own room. I just thought it was one of the nicest things."

When college acceptance letters came, his best choices were two universities in Philadelphia. However, neither school offered enough aid for him to be able to attend. To Michael's great good luck, board member Marnie Christian was overseeing the college application process for both seniors that year, and she had good local contacts. Now she stayed in almost daily phone contact with admissions and aid people at both schools to see if they could cobble together an improved package for Michael.

I was worried about how Michael was holding up under all this stress and uncertainty. His housemate, Elvis, the other senior, had known where he was going for months. At the time, I was dropping by the ABC House a few times a week after school to touch base with whoever of the boys were hanging around. Now, every time I came, I found Michael sitting in the living room passively watching TV. Concerned, I tried several times to engage him in conversation about his worries. He simply replied, "I have faith in Marnie." His faith was well placed. I don't know who eventually pulled a rabbit out of the hat, but one of the schools offered Michael an excellent aid package, which enabled him to attend and graduate majoring in business.

Michael said, "Staying in Philadelphia was one of the best decisions I ever made, only because I am closer to Rex and Meg in a physical sense. As I have left ABC, we are even closer now." From the perspective of his senior year in college he said, "I've known them for seven years. I consider them my two greatest friends and allies in the world. Every major decision, every major problem that I have, I run it by them. I speak to them constantly, almost on an everyday basis. They make so much sense in the advice they give me."

He went on to say that he feels a part of their extended families and, "They are honestly part of my family now. I would say we were definitely meant to be together."

Anthony: Art or Business

I don't remember why Marjorie Merklin and I decided to share helping Anthony with his college applications, but several times one or the other of us wondered aloud how we would have survived without each other. Marjorie took responsibility for getting Anthony—never the most prompt of teenagers—to his appointments with college counselor Jim Nolan; helped him sort out choices of colleges to apply to; and checked that all the details in his applications were taken care of. Anthony was careful about details in his paintings, but in the rest of his life, details needed to take care of themselves.

When I offered to help Anthony with his application essays, I could not have imagined how stressful this was going to be. The problems rested only partly with Anthony. Many adults in the ABC family like to be involved in the college selection and application process, and give valuable help, which can include suggesting colleges, taking students to visit campuses, and sometimes providing helpful contacts. Many also want to put in their two bits about the common application essay.

Anthony thought it would be helpful to get as many opinions as he could about his essay. Several men who were on the board, or married to board members, were only too happy to oblige. Of course, each person he talked to had definite and different ideas about what he should write about. Some even drafted whole paragraphs for him to use. At the time, Anthony was not a strong writer, and he struggled to write several different essays, seemingly trying to please the last person he talked to, after the one before that. As the weeks wore on, he became more and more confused, and I became more and more frustrated. I would call Marjorie just to cry on her shoulder.

By this time I had been Anthony's academic advisor since he joined our program, and knew him well. I finally managed to get him to settle on a topic, and with help from Jim Nolan, got him to finish one essay.

Marjorie and I suggested that he apply to some art schools, as it was clear he had both talent and an intense passion for drawing and painting. While he had mulled over various career possibilities, now he was steadfast in saying that he wanted to go into business. He told us that it is hard to make a living as an artist. He had grown up poor, and wanted to find a route to middle-class comfort. I kept unspoken my concern that unless Anthony's dreamy approach to life and his attitude toward deadlines changed, he could wind up a businessman who was poor. We all agreed that he should include slides of some of his artwork as part of his application package.

Anthony applied to the College of Arts and Sciences at Syracuse University, but someone in its admissions department must have recognized the talent that we saw. They admitted him, with a good scholarship, but to their College of Visual and Performing Arts. When we arranged for Anthony to visit to be sure he liked it, Tyrell, who was then a junior at Syracuse and who had never met him, rearranged his work schedule to host him. He introduced him to several of his friends and put him up in his dorm room. Anthony returned from this trip enthusiastic about Syracuse.

Lower Merion High School requires a senior experience project whereby seniors take their final exams early and then spend three weeks working on a project, exploring a topic approved by a guidance counselor or teacher. At the end of the period, the student gives a presentation about the project. Anthony chose to go to New York City, stay with an aunt, and visit art museums to see what he could learn about painting techniques.

First he visited the Metropolitan Museum of Art to study some old masters. He went to bookstores: "I used them as libraries to read up on the techniques I'd just seen." Then he worked on a few paintings that he had already done, modifying them from what he learned.

When he went to The Museum of Modern Art for the first time, Anthony became excited by whole areas of modern art which he had known little about. He painted several pieces in styles that he saw there.

Tim, one of the staff tutors, and I joined Anthony's guidance counselor for his presentation at the end of his project. Anthony started by telling us what he had learned at the Metropolitan, and then held up a portrait of his mother that he had modified. It had been a pleasant looking oil painting when I had seen it last, but now her eyes leapt off the canvas.

As he talked smoothly and enthusiastically about all the things he had seen at the museums and what he had learned, he held up his work, painting after painting, to illustrate what he was talking about. The three of us who were his audience sat mesmerized.

Postscript

When Anthony talked about taking a semester abroad his junior year at Syracuse, I urged him to look at programs in Florence, Italy. He signed up for one, and three weeks after he arrived I received an email, which is excerpted here:

> I went to the Uffizi today for the fifth time. It was amazing. I like the works of Caravaggio and Masaccio. I saw the Birth of Venus and it was the best painting I have seen in a while . . . I live two minutes away from Piazza San Marco, where the house of Fra

Angelico was. I will go there tomorrow. Today I tried gnocchi and hazelnut gelato. It was amazing . . . Today I also saw statue people. They look like famous sculptures but they are real people that stay still for long periods of time. Occasionally they move and scare people. Patty I am having the time of my life in Florence. I really love this city and the art.

Love, Anthony

Peter: Picking up the Pieces

When Peter was dismissed from the program, he was in the second semester of his senior year. If he were to finish high school at Lower Merion, he quickly had to find a place to live and a part-time job. Fortunately, Peter was a good friend of another senior at the high school, whose mother had been a student in another ABC program many years before. This woman kindly agreed to let Peter live with her family. Then Lisa Kahn, with whom he had stayed for two weeks, and two other board members, helped him move his things out of the ABC House.

Later I asked him, "When did the reality hit you?"

"As I was leaving," he answered. "I didn't care about leaving the house. But I realized I wasn't going to be with the guys anymore. I cried. Edwin cried, and Anthony. Once I left the house I wasn't going to be allowed to come back. It was tough."

Peter got a part-time job at a local pizza place washing dishes, and he eventually progressed to being oven man as well as handling the counter. His grades suffered badly, whether from the emotional turmoil, lack of the structure provided by the ABC program, or a case of senioritis, or all three. Fortunately, he had submitted all of his college applications by this time.

The board members who had been helping him with the college and financial aid process continued to do so. Several colleges accepted him, and Dickinson College gave him a good aid package. Lisa Kahn took time off from work to drive him to Carlisle in central Pennsylvania so he could visit Dickinson, and he decided to accept their offer.

When Jay and I interviewed him close to the end of the school term, I was pleased to hear him say, "I did this to myself." That was the first time I ever heard Peter accept clear responsibility for what he had done.

He graduated from high school on time. My favorite photo from that night is of him holding up a bright yellow happy face. The grin on Peter's face outshone the one on that yellow banner.

Wes Bradley came up with money for things Peter would need to start college. I joined Lisa Kahn one afternoon in late summer when she took Peter to shop for bedding, towels, and other dorm room necessities. A day or two later, Wes loaded up Peter and his things and drove him to Carlisle for college move-in day. He met Peter's roommate, and attended the first day events for parents. Wes came back enthusiastic about the college and about this new opportunity for Peter.

Reflections

Board members are always disappointed over dismissing a student from the program. However, for a complex set of reasons, not all of which I understand, Peter's dismissal caused more distress and dissension than usual. Several board members resigned shortly afterwards. It took several years to rebuild our board.

One of the disagreements centered on whether or not we should have dismissed Peter in his junior year and saved ourselves all the drama of his senior year. I, for one, am grateful we did not. Had Peter been sent home the spring of his junior year or at the end of that semester, he would have enrolled in an inner-city high school in Hartford, and had none of the structure and supports provided at ABC. Given Peter's impulsive nature, I'm not sure he would have even graduated from high school, let alone managed to get to a four-year college.

Edwin: Missing His Best Friends

One Sunday afternoon just before school started, I gave Jonathan and Denzel, who had been helping me garden, a ride back to Lisa Kahn's house. They were staying at her house during preseason cheerleading practice, along with Edwin. When we arrived, Lisa was on the phone—doing her best to locate Anthony, to urge him to get back to the U.S. and to start college on time. Anthony had traveled to the Dominican Republic to have a tonsillectomy. Already known for not getting to places on time, he now stood a good chance of being late to his first day at Syracuse.

When Lisa finally reached Anthony, Edwin took her phone. Standing in the driveway, alternately running his hands through his brown curls and thrusting his arm in the air in emphatic gestures, he talked in racecar-fast Spanish. I couldn't understand a word of it, but from his tone and hand gestures I imagined it translated as, "Dude! You've got to get back here. This is COLLEGE, man!"

After they finished talking, Edwin, looking upset and angry, told us that Anthony had not even had the surgery yet; it was scheduled for the next day. His ticket to fly back to Baltimore was for the following Sunday, three days after he was supposed to start school. "He's already been there two weeks. Why hasn't he had the surgery!" He explained that Anthony had traveled there for the surgery "because they treat us better there. But he needs to come back."

When he calmed down, I asked Edwin if he'd like to come over to my house to see Jay, who happened to be helping me out repainting our porch. Jay had left the ABC staff by then, and he'd just gotten a job teaching English at Harriton High

School, the other high school in the district. Edwin dashed into the house to change his shirt, and when we got to my house we told Jay about Anthony. Jay laughed and said, "That sounds so like Anthony."

I left Edwin and Jay alone for about half an hour. When I came out they were sitting on my patio steps and Edwin was giving Jay advice about how to get along with his students. "Just be yourself, man. If you treat 'em the way you treated us, they'll know you care."

When we got into my car to return to the Kahns', I gave Edwin a packet of photos I had taken at Anthony and Peter's graduation in June. "These are for you," I said.

He leafed through them rapidly, then again slowly. We had started out chatting, but now he was silent, studying each picture one by one. He reached up and turned the bill of his baseball cap from the back to the front. He kept turning the pictures. He pulled off his cap again and resettled the bill to the back.

I patted his knee and said, "They are your best friends, I know."

No words, just sniffles. He repositioned the cap a third time.

When we pulled into the Kahns' driveway I said, "Why don't we just sit here a few minutes?" Soon, Edwin was sobbing, pulling up the hem of his tee shirt to wipe his face. Finally, he turned in his seat, gave me a fierce hug, then collected himself enough to go into the house. Was he, I wondered, ready to face his senior year without the other two members of the Latin Lovers' Escort Service?

The next fall, Edwin followed Anthony to Syracuse University. If there was drama during his application process, I am not aware of it. Nine of the twelve colleges he applied to accepted him. However, Edwin faced one challenge the summer before he started school. Syracuse had admitted him to a special program, which required him to attend a precollege program on campus. He lived free in a dorm and had a meal allowance in a school cafeteria. The program didn't, however, provide any living allowance; Edwin, used to working in the summer, was short of spending money.

This situation seriously impacted his social life. Students he met in the program would say, "Let's go for a pizza," or "Let's go to a movie." Edwin would say, "Nah, I'm not hungry," or "Thanks, but I need to study." For someone as highly sociable as Edwin, I imagine this was a painful way to get started at college. He told me it was okay because he knew once school started in the fall, he'd have his aid package and his school-related job. Through the summer he got plenty to eat by having all of his meals in the cafeteria.

When school started, he was very happy to be placed in the same dorm as Anthony. The next year they roomed together. The following year Edwin, Anthony and some other young men shared an apartment.

Once when he was back visiting Ardmore, Edwin startled me by saying, "If you and Bob want to drive up to Syracuse sometime, you could stay with Anthony and me. You wouldn't have to pay for a hotel or nothing." Staying overnight in a messy apartment shared by several college-aged guys ranks very low in things I desire to do. Nevertheless, I rate it as one of the most endearing invitations I have ever received.

Jonathan: Senior Year—the Long Road to College

When Jonathan was going into his senior year, we no longer had a board member overseeing college applications, so I stepped up to shepherd him through the process. Jon took the SAT 1 exams in May after getting extensive one-on-one SAT tutoring, paid for by the ABC program.

Shortly before school let out in June, I took Jonathan for his first appointment with Jim Nolan to start the process of selecting colleges. Jon was excited and a bit nervous. Jim, a late middle-aged, soft bear of a man, greeted us by offering us sodas. Soon after he and Jonathan disappeared into Jim's office I could hear, through the closed door, Jonathan's loud, throaty laugh. This man, obviously, has a knack for putting teenagers at ease.

When they reappeared after an hour, Jonathan held a list of about thirty colleges to read up on over the summer. As we walked to my car, I asked to see it. The list contained a broad range of colleges including some I had never heard of. Meanwhile, Jonathan strutted to the car, singing all the while. I had never seen a kid so happy over starting the daunting process of applying to college. Jonathan had truly come a long way since he hid out at home to avoid bullies in his middle school.

I had talked to Jonathan several times about looking at Haverford College, which is located just a few blocks from the ABC House. I thought it was a reasonable-reach school for him, and because the admissions people there know our program, he probably stood a decent chance of being accepted. He had insisted he was not interested, saying, "When I graduate, I'm out of this town." Now, bringing him back to the ABC House, I swung my car onto the campus.

"Okay, Jon," I told him. "You're trapped in my car. Might as well look out the window."

"Patty, that's not fair!" But he looked. On our exit from the campus, he said, "Okay, you win. I'll look at Haverford."

A few days later I gave him a copy of *Fiske Guide to Colleges* to read over the summer. He was clearly anxious about writing his essay for the common application. I tried to reassure him, saying I would be there to lean on. I suggested he think over the summer about what theme to use in his essay.

On a Sunday afternoon in early September, I went over to the ABC House to help Jonathan with his essay. Pleasantly surprised to find he had already started on it, I sat in the living room and read a book while he worked in the computer room. Finally, he gave me a draft—too long—but it was not bad for a start. We had agreed he should build the essay around his quitting school in sixth grade and move on to how his seventh-grade teacher had convinced him he could change his life if he worked hard. That offered an easy segue into coming to ABC and the many challenges he'd met here.

After a detailed critique, I sent him back to the computer and went back to my book. Another revision—better, and then another. About three hours after we started, he had a decent draft. By this time we were both relaxed, laughing and joking. Suddenly, Jonathan became serious, turned his face half away and said, "Time out. I'm having an emotional moment."

Thinking he was being dramatic, I was about to make a joke when I looked at him and saw a mist of tears. "What is it?" I asked.

"I'm going to college. I really am."

Before I left, I cautioned him not to pass his essay around to a lot of people until it was finished. Jim Nolan would give him helpful comments, and Jon wanted to show it to his junior year English teacher, who had written a wonderfully positive letter of recommendation for him. I thought those two were fine. But I knew from past experience that lots of people want to be involved in this stage of the process, weigh in with critiques, and, at least in Anthony's case, it had confused him hugely. No way did I want a repeat of that.

The next day Jonathan called me and, in an excited voice, said how much his former English teacher liked his essay. Then came another phone call to tell me someone else had liked it.

At Jonathan's next appointment with Jim Nolan, he took along his transcript. Jim read it as they walked into his office and, as the door was closing, I overheard him say, "Well, these grades aren't too shabby." Surrogate parental pride flowed through me.

Jim, pleased with the essay, made a few suggestions for tweaking it. Over the course of the rest of the week, Jonathan kept calling to tell me how yet another friend or teacher loved what he was now calling, "my amazing essay." Then about a week later he called complaining, "These people are driving me crazy!" He had shown it to several board members and two or three of them had made extensive suggestions for changing it, including drafting additional paragraphs for him to add.

"Sweetie, I told you this would happen if you kept passing it around."

"Well, I'm not changing it!" he answered. I was glad that he had enough self-confidence to not try to please every single person.

During that time, Jonathan was also studying to retake the SAT I, hoping to raise his scores, which were just average. When he retook the exams, though, his scores barely budged. He'd have to rely on his excellent grades, including in many honor and AP classes, and on his being in the ABC program.

One day in mid-September, I picked Jonathan up after school and drove to the Haverford College campus so we could take the college tour together. While we waited for the guide, Jonathan immediately started chatting with other students waiting for the tour. When the student tour guide turned up, she proved to be an attractive and very outgoing young woman. Jonathan asked lots of questions and, at the end of the tour, he told her she had sold him on Haverford. Whether he was sold on the college or just on the girl, Haverford went on his list.

Jonathan met with Jim Nolan every two weeks for the next few months and by sometime in October, they had pruned his college list to eleven schools, including four state universities in New England. His reach schools were Bowdoin, Cornell, Dartmouth, Haverford and Wesleyan. Miami and Boston Universities rounded out his list.

Five of the schools required a second essay in addition to the one for the common application. So began our regular Sunday afternoon routine. He struggled with an essay for Boston University, realization dawning on him that the hurdle of writing the common application essay was not to be the only one. I wasn't worried because I knew that Jonathan is an extraordinarily well-organized and responsible person. He was doing a splendid job of keeping track of all the details for his many applications, and was making contacts with admission representatives at the various schools he was applying to.

I went by the ABC House on another Sunday afternoon to help Jonathan on his second special essay. He greeted me by saying he already had a draft of his essay for Bowdoin. I read it and my heart sank. Written in a flowery style, totally unlike his common application essay, it was almost devoid of content. The theme centered on his imagining himself at Bowdoin on an autumn afternoon being happy and admiring fall colors. Seeing how excited and pleased he was with it, I thought, *this is going to be a long afternoon*. I made several suggestions and told him to rewrite it. I sat at a desk reading a book while he worked at the computer for a half hour or so. This version, a tiny bit better, but not much. We did another round of critique and rewriting. This time I got more assertive and started striking out adjectives. Offended, Jonathan asked, "What don't you like about it?"

"It reads like you never met an adjective you didn't like," I said, asking what gave him the idea to write in that style, so different from the way he usually writes.

"Ever since I read *The Great Gatsby*."

Oh, Lord. An F. Scott wannabe. I told him he was only allowed one adjective per noun, max. He started calling me Word Chewer. The next version was quite a bit better, but I made more suggestions. He turned back to the computer and made changes.

"Okay, let me see it," I said.

"No! It's done."

"Oh, come on, Jon. Let me see it."

"No! Lady, go home." He turned his back on me and started trolling the Internet. I walked myself to the door, my tail between my legs. It was the only time ever that Jonathan didn't escort me to the door and give me a parting hug. Oh, well, I thought, he'll be recovered by next weekend when he has the next one to write.

The next day I got home about five and checked my email, which included a frantic request from Jonathan for information about voting machines, for a class assignment that was due the next day. I was forgiven.

The next Sunday he tackled a 250-word essay for the University of Maine, the only state university he had applied to that required an additional essay. Took a few hours. Later he called me to say he felt stupid. He hadn't read the instructions carefully enough; they wanted 250 characters not words. I laughed. So much for that Sunday afternoon.

Writing essays for Haverford and Cornell consumed two more Sunday afternoons for us, and then he was done. By early December he had sent in his applications to all eleven schools, well ahead of deadlines. I felt he deserved a celebration for all of his hard work and for staying on task so efficiently, and wanted to do something I was sure he would remember. I told him that my husband and I were taking him out to dinner, and encouraged him to invite along Samantha, one of the staff tutors whom he was especially close to. I didn't tell either of them where we were going. When we reached the entrance to a nearby Moroccan restaurant, Jonathan initially looked shocked when he saw pictures of belly dancers posted by the door. When the food arrived he was squeamish about not having forks and spoons, but he soon relaxed enough to both eat with gusto and to get up and dance with a couple of the belly dancers—a very satisfactory evening.

Somebody else was supervising Jonathan's financial aid application process. Jonathan and I had put in an intensive three months together, but now I, at least, could relax. My part was done—or so I thought.

A Few Bumps Along the Way

Just before winter break I took Jonathan with me for the quarterly parent-teacher conferences at the high school. The first several conferences went smoothly—as usual, he was doing very well in his classes. His English teacher, an alumnus of Haverford College, spent most of the conference telling him what a great school it is and encouraging him to go there. Afterwards, as we walked down a long hallway on the way to the next conference, Jonathan linked his arm through mine and said, "We've had lots of interesting times together this year." What a cozy, mellow moment I thought.

At the next conference, his AP Government teacher passed me printouts of his grades. Jonathan had given me no warning, nary a peep. His grade at that point was a D, and he was in danger of flunking the class. What in the world was going on? I turned toward Jonathan: he looked embarrassed, as if he wished he were any place but here. When I recovered from my shock, I pressed his teacher to explain what he thought was wrong, and what we could do about it. He told me that Jonathan was doing his homework, but was flunking or nearly flunking his exams.

When we asked Jonathan for his thoughts, he said he didn't like the class. Honest, but hardly tactful. Then he burst out in a bitter tone, "My family are immigrants. We don't sit around the dinner table talking about politics like the other kids' families do."

After we left the conference I told Jonathan, "This really matters. This will hurt you with competitive colleges." Jonathan acted as if he didn't want to hear about it; didn't want to even think about it. I've worked with enough ABC students over the years to recognize the signs of massive denial, but it was the first time I had seen it in Jonathan. And it was a critical time. The next quarter's grades, at the end of January, would be the last ones colleges saw before they made admission decisions. I told him I would tutor him in government when he got back after Christmas break. Since he was leaving for home the next day, I stopped chiding him and tried to make the rest of the evening a pleasant one.

I did what I usually do when the boys stump me: I called Mary Storey, whom I had worked with on the boys' academic programs for many years. Her knowledge about kids and her good sense about handling them are immense. She agreed that the best plan was for me to undertake some intensive tutoring when Jonathan got back, and she offered to find review materials for him. I bought a copy of the supplemental reading: Hedrick Smith's *Power Game*, a big fat paperback, and spent part of the Christmas break reading hunks of it.

At our post-conference academic committee meeting in early January, five or six board members and academic advisors sat in the cluttered house office discussing the boys' school progress. I related what had happened in Jonathan's government conference, and my sense that he was still trying to blow it and me off. "I think we need to pull him in here and intimidate him," I said.

Jonathan was not used to being brought into the office. He looked decidedly unhappy, but was polite as I sketched out my plan to work with him. When I left the house that evening, I took with me the textbook for his government class.

So began another set of Saturday or Sunday afternoon sessions together, as well as several hours a week during study hall. I grew up on the periphery of politics—my father, as part of his job, spent years lobbying in the California State legislature—and I have worked in many campaigns, and am a committed political junky. I told Jonathan, "If you had to be bombing a class, it was considerate of you to pick one that is so easy for me to help you with."

Jonathan buckled down and worked very hard. It quickly became clear that he had trouble retaining what he was reading. Floundering around for a way to make the material stick in his head, I started telling him stories, mostly from the rich lode of my father's experience in California politics. Since our immediate focus was an upcoming exam on lobbying and political influence, this was a natural.

In mid-January Jonathan had a unit test in AP Government. I was probably as nervous as he was about it. A few days later he called, his voice high, "Oh, my God, oh my God! I got a B on the AP Gov. test."

We kept up our intense schedule of tutoring until after midterms. By the end of the month I realized that the reason the class was so difficult for Jonathan lay in just what he had told us. He was an immigrant child whose family rarely discussed political topics. He had no vocabulary or common set of concepts in which to frame the subject matter of the class—something most of the other students did have. I told him, it must be like a non-Hispanic kid taking third year Spanish without having taken first and second year. In retrospect, we shouldn't have let him sign up for this AP class, even though his AP U.S. History teacher had recommended that he take it.

Jonathan managed to pull his grade up to a C for the end of the semester. He and I laughed about the anomaly of his being happy to get a C. Mary and I suggested that he change to a standard-level class for the second semester of the required government class. To no one's surprise, Jonathan opted to continue in the AP class, and agreed to keep working with me, although not as intensely. He is anything but a quitter.

Soon he started hearing from colleges. I got an excited phone call from him to say he had been accepted to the University of New Hampshire. Then came a rejection from Boston University and another from the University of Miami. He was getting nervous, even though he soon received acceptances from all of the state universities he had applied to. I was worried, because I was pretty sure that scholarship money at state schools was not going to be enough for him to attend. There would be no money from home.

He did have his college deposit money in hand. Or rather, I had it. He had given me money he had saved to hold so he wouldn't be tempted to spend it. Four hundred dollars was sitting in a drawer in my house.

Then one afternoon in late March, my phone rang. Jonathan was so excited I could barely understand him. "I got into Haverford. Haverford College!" Two days later, another phone call. "I got into Bowdoin. Isn't that amazing?"

"Aren't you glad that I made you rewrite the Bowdoin essay four or five times?"

I shouldn't have rubbed it in. Fortunately, Jonathan didn't take offense. Bowdoin's acceptance included a financial aid package. Several days later he got an acceptance from Wesleyan University. Three wonderful colleges.

By now I had begun to realize we might have a serious problem with the aid process. That fall, Jonathan and his mother had provided all the income information required to the small company that processed financial paperwork for our seniors. But now they needed to process this year's income tax information. Jonathan's mother was slow in getting it to him, and then the process slid to a halt. Having been assured that experts were dealing with this, I had put it out of my mind. When Jonathan told me that the colleges didn't have his information yet, I was floored. I called the contact person at the company repeatedly before she finally returned my call. It was only weeks before he had to give colleges his answer.

I got the impression that this young woman was swamped with her workload, and that Jonathan's paperwork was still sitting on her desk. If she didn't have time to do this, she should have let us know. I could have figured out how to do it and done it for him. Now, since I had none of the necessary information, I could only push her to please, please, please get it off to Haverford and Wesleyan and forget the other schools. Bowdoin, bless them, had based their aid offer on the previous year's data.

My feelings oscillated between sick and furious. Jonathan had worked so very hard while he was with us, all four years, and was on the verge of having some wonderful options. How could one person's carelessness jeopardize his future? I fumed to anyone who would listen, "If I don't have a nervous breakdown by May first, it'll be a miracle!"

Jonathan had visited both Haverford and Wesleyan the previous fall, and had especially liked Wesleyan. Now we thought he should look at Bowdoin. Bowdoin's admissions office arranged and paid for him to visit on a weekend trip in mid-April for accepted students. The day he was to come back, he called to say the college was snowed in, so he had to stay an extra day, and everybody was so nice, and he was having a wonderful, wonderful time. "I'm coming to Bowdoin."

"I'm glad you like it so much, but we'll talk about it when you get home."

"Nope! I'm coming to Bowdoin."

"Jon, I have your deposit money. We'll talk about it when you get back."

"Patty, that's not fair. Oh, all right . . . But I'm coming to Bowdoin."

My hesitation rested on his tendency to be very positive about many new experiences; and I wanted him to reflect on it a little, especially since he had been almost equally positive about Wesleyan when he visited that in the fall. On the other hand, so far Bowdoin was the only school that had offered financial aid. Jonathan and I talked a few days after he got back. He was sure that Bowdoin was what he wanted. Having forced him to sleep on it, I gave him a check for his deposit. He bubbled all over. I felt, whew!

In early May I drove to the ABC House after school to take Jonathan to pick up his tux for the prom, which was two days away. He was taking the girl he had described all year as his best friend. She was also the girl he measured all others against, to have them come up wanting. As we headed off to the King of Prussia Mall, he suddenly said, "This is the best time of my life."

"How is that?"

"I'm going to college. I'm going to Bowdoin! And I'm going to the prom."

I couldn't cry: I was driving.

CHAPTER 10

Coda

Charles

After Charles graduated from an Ivy League university, he taught in a middle school close to the neighborhood where he grew up and earned a master's degree in education. He then returned to school and earned the law degree he had long dreamed of. Most recently he was working on a graduate law degree—quite a change from being stuck in a vocational school so many years ago.

Tyrell

Tyrell attended a Summer Start program at Syracuse University before his freshman year. There he met a fellow freshman, Deon, a young woman who was also from New York City. For the next year or so they were just acquaintances, but during their sophomore year, "We started hanging out together." He told his mother, "She's the one! I'm going to marry her." His mother pointed out he was only nineteen years old, so how could he know? Tyrell reports that when his mother met Deon, she loved her. "My whole family loved her."

Tyrell graduated in management and finance from Syracuse in 2006 and moved back home for a few years. In April 2007 his mother died in her sleep at age fifty-five of heart disease. His father had died of complications from diabetes during Tyrell's freshman year in college, so by his early twenties he had lost both parents, although he still had three sisters, including his twin, and a brother.

Tyrell's financial aid package at Syracuse included the expectation of his earning money from a campus job and summer employment. During the summer after his first year, he was unable to find a job in New York City, so he worked extra hours the next school year at his campus job. The following summer he got a summer job through Deon's mother's contacts. He had to travel by subway an hour each way, and was paid minimum wage. By this time he worked at a campus job as a security desk person in a campus dorm during the school year. This allowed him to do some of his homework on the job, and he worked many hours while keeping up with his schoolwork.

The following summer he secured an internship with Target in New York City, and on graduation took a job with them as an executive team leader for replenishment and was later promoted to being an assistant store manager. He worked in a busy Target store in the same neighborhood in Brooklyn where he had grown up. He stayed there for over six years and then took a job as a store manager with a large Toys "R" Us, Inc. Recently, he accepted a position as an assistant store manager at Macy's Herald Square, Macy's flagship store.

He was doing as well in his personal life. Deon had majored in psychology at Syracuse, and then earned a master's in social work at NYU. She now works as a social worker at a hospital in Brooklyn. A couple of years after Tyrell's mother died, he and Deon moved in together; they married a few years later. At nineteen Tyrell had known his heart's desire. A boy who had grown up in a loving family with two supportive parents was launched into the career and personal life that surely his parents must have hoped for him.

Elvis

Elvis graduated from Haverford College in art, specializing in photography, a few months before the country's economy fell off a cliff. He worked for a Haverford faculty member that summer, and I saw him several times when he helped me in my garden for some extra money. He seemed happy, in love with his college sweetheart. He rescued me that summer when my rose arbor collapsed a few weeks before my daughter's wedding. He helped me select a sturdier one, then, with me assisting, assembled it, including embedding it in concrete. I was impressed with his competence and confidence—all the years helping his father construct pigeon coops showed. For me, the rose arbor held a special connection to Elvis. When he was a high school sophomore, he had helped me plant roses for the arbor. As I was trimming some of the roses from the shrubs, he asked if he could have a few. He planned to visit his girlfriend who lived in a suburb several miles west the next day, and wanted to give them to her. I was happy to oblige. Ever since, I treasure the mental image I have of a big, muscular fifteen-year-old riding the Paoli Local suburban train, with his fist clutching a jam jar full of peachy-pink roses.

At the time, years later, when Elvis put in the new arbor, I am sure he had no idea, nor did I, how difficult the job market was about to turn.

In the fall, Elvis secured a visitor's services job at the Philadelphia Museum of Art. He was living with his sweetheart, a young woman he thought he would marry. Partway through that first post-college year, she broke up with him. Heartbroken, he decided to move back to New York for a fresh start. He intended to "hit the ground running" by applying for a management position at the Metropolitan Museum of Art.

While waiting to hear from the Met, he began working for a scaffolding company where he'd had a summer job in college. Then the Whitney Museum of American Art called, offering him the same visitor services job he had in Philadelphia, but this was only part time. He accepted, and was glad he had when he did not get the Met job.

For three months, he worked seven days a week between the museum and scaffolding jobs. But when his schedule at the Whitney changed, he had to choose between the two. He decided to stay with the scaffolding job, which was full time and paid more. Six months later, the scaffolding company was sold and moved to another state. "I could have made things work, but part of me was still not satisfied with what I was doing. Things were pretty down for me for a bit."

While Elvis was in college, his mother had accepted a job at Disney World, and his parents and two of his siblings moved to Florida. His father had been on disability since having a serious accident when Elvis was in high school. Now, he said, his mother urged him to "move back home to Florida, go back to school, and start over. Her offer was my chance to find a fulfilling career, and what better karma booster is there in the world than the medical profession?" He enrolled in an EMT program at a community college. After having struggled through chemistry when he was in high school, he found that earning his EMT certification pumped up his confidence a lot. "My thinking was that after gaining that, the only dream I held on to and was always too scared to see through was serving my country."

Disney World called him for an interview about the time he finished the EMT course. He felt he'd had enough of dealing with patrons in his museum jobs, "so I thought what job would keep me away from guests? Hence, I became a janitor." The first three days of his employment he had to attend a seminar on how to interact with the guests.

After he got his EMT certificate, Elvis looked for jobs with hospitals, but he also began to seriously consider the military path. In early 2012 he enlisted in the Navy. He imagined joining as a medic, but he did not want to wait as long as it would take for that opening. Even then, he had to wait nine months to go to boot camp, while continuing to work as a janitor at Disney.

As of early 2014, Elvis was serving as a third class Petty Officer deployed on the *USS Carney*, a guided-missile destroyer, and trained as a cryptologic technician. He sounded much happier than he had two years earlier. Shortly after the ship returned to homeport in May, Elvis was promoted to be a second class Petty Officer. As of early 2015, he was serving on the USNS *Spearhead* for an Africom deployment.

I think joining the Navy was a wise decision on Elvis's part. He was a strong, natural leader among his ABC housemates. I hope that being in the Navy will allow those qualities to reemerge and flourish.

Michael

Michael, who attended a university in the Philadelphia area, graduated with a degree in business. He worked part-time at a local business for the last two years of his studies. That business hired him full time when he graduated. Initially, he worked in the finance department, but, after a year of full-time work, he was promoted to sales, where he continues. His job in college and his major helped him avoid the employment pitfalls that hampered the dreams of so many of his age mates.

Michael was one of the ABC students who, at one point, had crushes on the singer Alicia Keyes—strong enough that he wrote a poem about her. While still in college he fathered a daughter—who is named Alicia.

Two and a half years after graduating from college, Michael was living in his own house in South Philadelphia, sounding content. His friendship with his host parents remained unusually close.

Anthony

Anthony managed to graduate from Syracuse University in four years, in spite of changing his major twice: first from painting to liberal arts, and then to computer arts with a minor in advertising. But he graduated in May 2009 smack into a bad recession. He moved to New York City and stayed with a cousin for six months while he looked for a job in advertising. No luck. "They were into firing, not hiring." So he moved back home to Baltimore for three months, and made a little money doing photo shoots of "friends of friends." Meanwhile he sent emails to production companies in Los Angeles and Hollywood. One responded, so Anthony moved to the Los Angeles area and took a one-year internship as an assistant to a director of music videos.

When that ended, he returned to Baltimore. After a couple of months, "on a whim, I returned to LA." There he found a job with a mid-sized advertising firm as a junior art director and junior project manager on video game accounts. He worked there for nine months, until the director he had interned for helped him get a job with a startup Latino TV channel, which will target young, bilingual, U.S.-born Hispanics. The company is under the umbrella of a major, established firm. Anthony said, "I love it. It's fast paced. I'm running around all over town, going to meetings. I get to use my art talent for visual creativity." Recently Anthony has traveled to Mexico, Puerto Rico, Russia and his native Dominican Republic on video shoots. He described himself as "working like a horse," but sounded happy and alive.

Anthony, whose driving interest is visual and artistic, has carved out a career path consistent with his talents and his passion, and he has done so during an economy stacked against him.

Peter

Peter selected international business and management as his major at Dickinson, and joined the cheerleading team. He lasted through almost two years of college, but dropped out before the end of his sophomore year. He later told me, "I wasn't mentally prepared for college and was partying too much. I dropped out before I flunked out. I just couldn't function without the structure that ABC provided."

The young woman who was now his girlfriend graduated that spring, and Peter followed her to Albany, New York. There he worked at a rental center for about a year until he grew sick of it, walked into a recruiting center and signed up for the Army.

This move should not have surprised me. At the start of Peter's senior year in high school he had met up with a Marine recruiter at a local gym, and that young man pursued Peter. I remember a staff tutor and I both cautioning Peter against joining the military at that point—he needed to finish high school and go to college.

After basic training, Peter spent five months at Fort Leonard Wood, training to be an MP. When Peter told me he would be a member of the military police, so help me, I laughed. I don't think he appreciated my reaction.

Shortly before he was deployed to Iraq, where the United States still had an active combat presence, he married his college sweetheart, with Edwin serving as his best man. After a year in Iraq he returned to Fort Bliss, Texas. Upon leaving the service, he enrolled at the University of Texas El Paso branch, where he studied accounting. Peter said, "Then life threw me a couple of curve balls but I'm adapting." He moved to Queens, New York, and is working as a Veteran's Navigator for Samaritan Village, helping to connect veterans with services and homes if they are homeless.

My impression is that Peter was trying to regroup and decide what should be the next step in his life. It brought to mind the last two lines of a poem he wrote as a high school freshman.

So my mind and body are still on the search,
The search for a place that I can call HOME.

Edwin

When Edwin was applying to get into the ABC program, he rose early on a Saturday morning to take a standardized test required as part of his application. Several of his friends had talked about going, too, but decided they didn't want to get up that early. This situation repeated itself when Edwin was close to the end of university.

Edwin loved his major, international relations, but when the recession hit in 2008, he started to worry. People graduating in his major were not getting jobs. He decided to reevaluate his goals. One of his fraternity brothers had done a summer internship at JP Morgan Chase, which led to a job with them; so, in the spring of 2010, Edwin decided to go to a career fair at Syracuse. Several of his friends planned to go with him but backed out, saying, "They'll just want people majoring in finance, business or technology." Even his roommate backed out at the last minute.

When Edwin got to the fair he walked right to the JP Morgan Chase table. There he talked to a recruiter, who told him they were only looking for finance and technology majors. Edwin started chatting with her, "just being myself." After a while he asked her to look at his resumé and give him advice on it. She was especially interested in his jobs at college and during summers when he was in high school. Meanwhile, a line formed behind him and he told her, "Shouldn't you be talking to these people?" She replied, "I'm talking to you."

Later that evening, she sent him a text message asking what he was doing at noon the next day. "I had a quiz in a poly sci class then, but I said I had nothing and could meet her." That night his fraternity brother gave him a crash course about JP Morgan Chase. At the interview the next day, the recruiter asked two questions: Why JP Morgan, and why you? Edwin said he was well prepared. The recruiter told him she was recommending him for an internship, but the decision would be up to the human resources department. Somewhat later, he got a phone call offering him a ten-week internship in the summer. At the end of the internship, his manager asked him to extend it. Then he got interviewed for a job, and was offered a full-time position when he finished school the following spring. The day he got the job offer, he was home in New York for the weekend. His mother started screaming with excitement. The person from human resources told Edwin it was the most exciting call she had made for some time. The next June, he started his job as an asset management analyst. By 2014 he had been promoted to Associate in the Mortgage Bank in JP Morgan Chase. That same year, he married a young woman he'd met in the summer of 2008 while he was working at a summer camp for kids in Central Park.

At thirteen years old, Edwin went to take a test and ended up as an ABC Scholar. Graduating from college into a bad economy, once again Edwin stepped up, took a risk and secured an excellent beginning job.

Jonathan

At the high school award ceremony just before he graduated, Jonathan was pleasantly surprised to be awarded a scholarship from Pacifico, a local company, which carried a grant of $1,000 for his college expenses. Jonathan began as an environmental studies major at Bowdoin College in Brunswick, Maine, in the fall of 2007. During spring break of his freshman year, he came back to Ardmore for a visit, and spent one night with us. He loved college and was excited about his courses. He and I stayed up late talking about issues he had discussed in a class in sociology. While it is heartwarming to see our students moving on to secure careers and, hopefully, middle-class incomes, it was a rare treat for me to chat with one of them who was so enthusiastic about intellectual ideas.

I reluctantly called a halt about one in the morning, not able to keep up with an undergraduate.

On that visit he also told me he had decided to take a double major, with Spanish as the second one. He said there were few Latinos at Bowdoin, and he thought doing this would help him maintain his culture.

Starting in Jonathan's second year at Bowdoin, he had two campus jobs. One was as a telecommunications assistant that brought with it the extra benefit of a supervisor—a retired chief in the United States Navy—who became a strong and supportive role model. Jonathan worked at this job through the next two summers as well. He told me that being poor at Bowdoin was harder than at ABC. Many of his classmates didn't understand why he worked so many hours at campus jobs, and didn't go on many weekend outings. He was uncomfortable telling them he just couldn't afford to.

During spring break of his junior year, he flew to Puerto Rico and visited the small town, Santa Isabel, where he had lived as a child. He visited relatives, including his paternal grandmother, whom he had not seen since he moved back to the United States when he was eleven. He was welcomed everywhere.

Jonathan wrote a senior independent study thesis on several Latin American poets, including Julia de Burgos of Puerto Rico. This both impressed and amused me, since his high school Spanish teacher, Mrs. Nemoy, and I had had to do some arm-twisting to get him to sign up for AP Spanish. He had complained he didn't really like literature that much. At Bowdoin he took several Spanish literature classes, and loved them.

Jonathan starting consulting the college career development office early in his junior year, a year earlier than most students do. He graduated from Bowdoin in May 2011, into a job market that was still sputtering. Within two months he had secured a job with a reinsurance firm in South Portland, Maine. His fluency in Spanish turned out to have a major benefit—two of the clients that his group managed are companies in Puerto Rico. By three and a half years into the job, he had been promoted twice and had earned two professional designations in his field. He was working as a Long-Term Disability (LTD) Claims Examiner II. He wrote, "I'm moving up in the insurance world, Patty!" The young man, who had dropped out of school in the sixth grade, was launched onto a very different and promising life path.

Appendix

OUR METHODS

The material for this book comes from three sources: poems and essays by ABC students, my and Jay's personal recollections, and extensive taped interviews with eight boys.

Jay and I conducted some of the interviews together. However, the majority I did alone, sometimes with one boy, sometimes with two or three in the same conversation. We owe a debt to Elvis and Michael, as the first interview we undertook was with them jointly, one Friday evening when they were high school seniors. They were house leaders at the time, and we feel that their willingness to talk to us about their experiences in the program legitimized our project with the younger boys. Jay had been a well-liked staff member for three years, and we began the interviews the year after he left the staff. Although the boys all knew me because I had been an active board member for many years, I think Jay's involvement in the beginning made them more comfortable talking to me.

While we did many interviews that winter and spring, I also had the luxury of going back during the next few years to talk with individual boys, as the topics we wanted to address evolved. In addition, Elvis and Michael both attended college in the Philadelphia area, so I was able to talk to each of them while they were in college. Jonathan and Edwin both visited Ardmore while they were in college, and I was able to talk with them when they were here.

Charles and Tyrell were both in college when we started the project. Each graciously came down from New York for an overnight visit with me, and we talked for hours. However, they are the only ones with whom I was not able to go back and to expand on what I had from earlier interviews.

In the parts of the book that are based on the interviews, I have been insistent on using the boys' own words. Nothing has been changed or made up to make it more grammatical, in spite of suggestions from some writing colleagues. However, when a person's name mentioned in a quote is an alias, I have changed the quote to reflect that.

Many of the chapters are reconstructed scenes. Some of these are from events I was directly involved in, some are from Jay's experience, and some are based on what boys told us in interviews. In all of these, dialogue is reconstructed from memory or from what I was told by Jay or the boys. However, no events are made up and there are no characters that are composites. Several recent scandals over memoirs and journalistic feature articles where events or persons are invented have called into question the legitimacy of the memoir genre. While this book is not a sociological research study, I have tried to be faithful to norms of honesty.

Six of the eight principal ABC scholars who are subjects in the book chose to have their real names used. Two (Charles and Michael) requested pseudonyms, and I have given fewer identifying details for them. Most of the ABC students who are minor characters have pseudonyms, as do other friends of the boys. Names of some adults in the book are also pseudonyms.

I owe a special thanks to the staff member referred to as Dean, who was one of the resident directors when I undertook the early interviews. He graciously invited me to come to dinner at the house once a week while the staff was sequestered having their weekly staff meeting over dinner. On those nights I was the one adult at dinner with the boys, chatting with them, then luring one or two to talk to me on tape between the end of dinner and the start of study hall. It proved an enjoyable and efficient way to get the interviewing done. Because 1 was coming for dinner, 1 brought freshly baked brownies with me each time. 1 am now known among the boys in the program, current and past, as "the brownie lady."

Acknowledgments

First, a huge thank you to the eight young men who generously shared their stories with us. I hope that I have faithfully represented their experiences as A Better Chance (ABC) Scholars.

Another thank you to the staff members who facilitated our interviewing the boys, and for all the commitment they brought to mentoring a houseful of teenagers, year after year. Hayat Omar gave especially warm support to our project.

We also owe our thanks to the many, many adults who together make our ABC program work. A few board members and host parents are featured in this book, but they are only a small fraction of the people who volunteer their time and talents to the program and to the students in it.

I wish to acknowledge special help and support from my ABC colleagues Diane Nissen, Mary Storey, and Marjorie Merklin. Sharon Sherman and Curt Wilson were my mentors when I first joined the ABC board and I owe them immeasurably. Sharon was the photographer for some of the pictures used in the book and for the cover and she generously allowed us to use them. Gary Schildhorn graciously gave me legal advice on several issues with the book, and I am grateful to him. The man whose pseudonym is Wes Bradley has been a compatriot and friend through all the years I have worked with the program, and my debt to him is great.

My editor, Miriam Seidel, became my guardian angel. She figured out how to organize a disparate collection of stories into a coherent narrative. And she has added to the book in other ways large and small and too numerous to detail.

Doug Gordon not only designed the book, he also guided me, with patience and good humor, through many decisions and choices about producing the book.

Carole Fowler's warm encouragement at an early point when I was stuck was critical for my sticking with the project. I owe thanks to Dr. Dorothy Wolfe for thoughtfully reading the entire manuscript and for listening to me worry about it for years. My lovely daughter, Dr. Maria Krisch, read individual pieces as I wrote them and then the entire manuscript a couple of times. Her careful and detailed comments and her support were invaluable.

I wrote most of this while I was a member of a writing workshop class taught by Virginia Newlin. Ginnie was especially helpful while I struggled to find a writing voice for this work, and I have learned so much from her over the years. I benefitted from many classmates' comments. I owe a special thanks to Jo Babich for her unending encouragement and many suggestions. I also owe thanks to the "writer's posse" Jo put together to help me for a critical piece. The posse members were Kristin Strid, Kate Varley and, of course, Jo herself.

I have long been grateful to Professor James F. Short, Jr., who introduced me to issues poor inner-city teenagers experience. Also, for his encouragement and fellowship support at a time when that was hard to come by for women graduate students.

My husband, Bob Krisch, solved all of my computer issues and cheered on this project from start to finish.

Without Jay Fritz, I could not have undertaken this. He is the source of many stories, and we undertook the initial interviews together. His other commitments did not allow us to write it as co-authors as we originally intended, but I am grateful for the two chapters he wrote. His enthusiasm for the project was unfailing.

ABOUT THE AUTHORS

Patricia Zita Krisch has been a board member of A Better Chance in Lower Merion for 20 years. She has a B.A. from Reed College and earned a Ph.D. in sociology from the University of Chicago, where she was a Woodrow Wilson Fellow. She worked as an academic research associate in demography and has taught courses in population and urban sociology as a university lecturer.

She has been active in local politics in Lower Merion Township, Pennsylvania, and served as a parent volunteer in the Lower Merion School District in several capacities, including as president of the Home and School Association of Lower Merion High School. She was appointed four times to school-district-wide committees: twice on long-range planning, once on reorganizing the high schools and once on revising social studies curriculum.

Jason S. Fritz is an award-winning poet. He was a residential tutor for two years, then a resident director for one year at ABC in Lower Merion. He earned a bachelor's degree from Haverford College and holds a Masters in Education from the University of Pennsylvania. He teaches English at Harriton High School in Lower Merion Township, Pennsylvania.

FOR MORE INFORMATION

Check our website, www.deasonpress.com, for more pictures and information about the book.

A Better Chance in Lower Merion is funded entirely by donations. If you would like to support its work, please send a check to:
    ABC in Lower Merion
    P.O. Box 213
    Ardmore, PA 19003
    www.abclowermerion.org

Contributions to the national A Better Chance program may be sent to:
    A Better Chance
    253 W. 35th Street, 6th Floor
    New York, NY 10001
    www.abetterchance.org

A history of the national A Better Chance program may be found in Zweigenhaft, Richard L., and G. William Domhoff, *Blacks in the White Elite: Will the Progress Continue?* (Lanham, MD: Rowman & Littlefield Publishers, Inc., 2003).